MIND
TRICKS

First published in 2007 by New Holland Publishers (UK) Ltd
London • Cape Town • Sydney • Auckland

1 3 5 7 9 10 8 6 4 2

www.newhollandpublishers.com

Garfield House, 86–88 Edgware Road, London W2 2EA, UK

80 McKenzie Street, Cape Town 8001, South Africa

Unit 1, 66 Gibbes Street, Chatswood, NSW 2067, Australia

218 Lake Road, Northcote, Auckland, New Zealand

ISBN 978 1 84537 743 4

Editorial Director: Jo Hemmings
Editor: Steffanie Brown
Artworks: Steve Crisp
Design and cover design: Ian Hughes, Mousemat Design Ltd
Production: Hazel Kirkman

Reproduction by Pica Digital PTE Ltd, Singapore
Printed and bound in China by Leo Paper Group

Note: The author and publishers have made every effort to ensure that the information given in this
book is accurate, but they cannot accept liability for any resulting loss or damage to either property or
person, whether direct or consequential and howsoever arising.

AUTHOR ACKNOWLEDGEMENTS

Firstly, my undying thanks to Steffanie and the whole team at New Holland for continuing
to help make my ideas a reality. I must also thank Steve Crisp, my good friend and a
brilliant artist, for another stunning job with his illustrations.

I must repeat my thanks to all the magicians who have inspired me, taught me and helped
me create my own magic in print and in reality over the years.
My special thanks to those who help by standing by me and keeping their
confidence in me – you know who you are!

Finally the biggest thank you of all goes to the most wonderful person I have ever met, my
wife Emma, who has given more to me in the last 25 years than
I could ever deserve.

MARC LEMEZMA'S
MIND TRICKS

MASTERING THE ART
OF MENTAL MAGIC

NH
NEW
HOLLAND

CONTENTS

Introduction 6

CHAPTER 1: SCORE WITH RAPPORT 10

CHAPTER 2: THE SIGNS ARE THERE 24

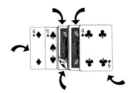

CHAPTER 3: UNDER THE INFLUENCE 40

CHAPTER 4: ANYTHING YOU CAN DO... 50

CHAPTER 5: ...I CAN DO BETTER! 62

CHAPTER 6: RIGHT FROM THE START 76

INTRODUCTION

I hope you're ready for this...
because I am going to make your head hurt!

A BRAVE NEW WORLD – MAYBE

In 2003 I published my first book on mind reading, or mentalism, that branch of the magical arts that deals with the reading of thoughts, the control of actions and physical objects and the prediction of choices, outcomes and events that have yet to occur. The popularity, public awareness and demand for this kind of 'magic' have grown immensely since then. This growth has been reflected in the success of that book, *Mind Magic*, which has now been reprinted and published in several languages.

I would not be so bold as to claim credit for creating that change in demand, of course; I was fortunate enough to have a good idea for a book at the right time. The stage had been set by the TV 'street magicians' of the late 1990s, who quite literally shocked the magic world into reinventing itself, making it more acceptable and palatable for modern audiences. The great irony was that nothing greatly original was needed to make this happen. These magicians simply stripped back all the formalities, threw away the crushed velvet suits and got back to where it all started – the streets!

This 'new context', complete with the help of some clever TV production techniques, changed the focus of magic from being solely on the performer, and diverted it towards those for whom we magicians were performing. We wanted to see the audience's reaction, and how the magic affected the viewers physically and emotionally. In essence, a new relationship was defined. No longer does an audience simply watch and react as a magician performs his act. The viewers have now become voyeurs, observing and dissecting the process (the cause, effect and aftermath), rather than just the performance.

WHAT'S IN A NAME?

There are many names given to this brand of magic, 'mentalism', 'mind magic' and 'mind reading' being the most popular. The term 'psychological magic' is also becoming quite popular, perhaps reflecting a style of presentation in which results are achieved through the use of psychological techniques, rather than via a magician's trickery. To keep things simple, we'll refer to this type of magic as 'mind magic' throughout this book. Of course, you may call it whatever you think suits your style and performance.

You might hear some mind magicians state that their results are achieved through a combination of 'magician's techniques, showmanship, misdirection and psychology'. This is undoubtedly true, but the implication that these magicians use more psychology in their show than a children's magician performing party tricks is most definitely not true. All magical performers use each of these elements in some combination or other. The difference is that in psychological magic, it is implied that 'psychology' is the main methodology.

It is this 'psychological' magic that has risen to the fore in recent years. It is not a new thing – it is simply part of a long cycle. If you give the subject some thought, you can see why psychological magic is so popular today: it fits perfectly with the concept of 'voyeurism', in which our society seems to be increasingly partaking (witness the rise in popularity of reality television shows). Indeed, this psychological approach will be the foundation of this book.

A REALITY CHECK

The psychological techniques that are implied in mind magic can and do work. It is possible to make generalized statements that individuals accept as being entirely personal and related to them. It is possible to predict in general terms the way groups of people will react to certain questions or prompts. It is also possible to tell something about a person's mood, the way they make choices and decisions, and even their feelings about you, using psychological techniques.

You can even influence them to make the 'choices' you wish them to.

Yet none of these techniques is entirely robust; they all have their limitations. They are even less reliable in a performance situation, which may be busy or noisy, and not conducive to building a strong rapport. If you need any more convincing, I suggest you take the time to go to watch a stage hypnotist perform live. He will go through a lengthy selection process at the start of his act to find those in his audience who are more suggestible than others. He is, in fact, improving his chances of success by eliminating 95 per cent of his audience from becoming involved with the substance of his act.

While it undoubtedly enhances a mind magic performance if there are a few minor errors or the odd 'miss' (it implies your abilities are in some way real and you have simply misread something or couldn't 'see' the full picture), simply relying on psychological techniques will not guarantee the success of your performance.

I earn my living entertaining and amazing my audiences, and thus I need solid, reliable techniques to ensure that my act works smoothly. Like most working magicians, I typically perform in a walk-around situation at functions. I approach a group, perform a few miracles and then move on to the next group. I have little choice about who I use in my act. In other words, I cannot rely on the subtler psychological techniques, but I do use them all the time – typically to enhance the effect of the trick.

The best opportunity to use psychological techniques occurs in a more formal stage or cabaret setting – on a stage, or even on television. Of course, to reach that kind of level takes years of work and study. You can start by studying this book, along with other good books and materials, and by observing and learning from (not copying or stealing from!) the work of other performers whom you admire.

AND SO THIS BOOK

In my previous book, *Mind Magic*, we explored the principles and techniques of mind magic, and dealt with its performance and emotional aspects in some great detail. The book actually caused great

controversy among magicians; some of them thought it was too good, giving away too much. But the majority applauded the work, some even regarding it as one of the best books on the subject. I was even promoted to a higher degree in the world-famous Magic Circle on the strength of that book!

I am not one to rest on my laurels, however, and so I feel I must take things a step further in this book. I want to teach my readers even more new tricks, effects and methods. The style of the tricks in this book is more 'psychological', but I am keen that the reader understands how this dimension is actually more about presentation than about the tricks themselves.

If you do own *Mind Magic*, you will know that in that book I used a distinct storytelling style to create the right atmosphere for trick performance. In this book, however, the style is more direct, reflecting the current trend towards a 'psychological' style. Another difference between the two books is that whereas in *Mind Magic*, everything you needed to perform the tricks could be found around your home or office, in this case I am going to ask you to pop along to your friendly local magic store and purchase a few tools.

In this book, my primary goal is to teach you how to replicate some of the more contemporary styles of mind magic. I hope that, after reading this book, you will be able to take virtually any effect from any magic book and, after some thought, time and practice, make it your own. Essentially, I hope to encourage you to study the magical arts in more depth, to help you find your own character, a unique style and a way of performing that suits your environment.

Enjoy!

CHAPTER 1:
SCORE WITH RAPPORT

I would like to begin this book with a brief story.

Occasionally, usually towards the end of an evening of performing magic, I am rewarded by a chance to revisit some of my audience. These are my favourite moments because I can build on the rapport that I have already established. Frequently the talk turns to the psychological aspects of magic, and I often conduct some 'pseudo-tests'. On one occasion I stunned a woman so deeply that I actually became worried that I had gone too far.

In demonstrating my skills, I had asked her to name her first boyfriend. This was in an attempt to learn her preferred communication style (more of which later). She gave me so much information in just half a second through her facial expressions that I was then able to give her the impression I had truly read her mind. And perhaps, in a way, I had. She answered my question, which allowed me to continue with my demonstration. Afterwards, I took her aside and revealed what she had inadvertently told me.

'I know that when you answered the question about your first boyfriend, you were not telling the truth. I believe that the person you named was the first boyfriend you took home to meet your parents, but that there was someone before.'

At this point, her jaw dropped to the floor.

'In fact, I think the person who you first loved was someone you shouldn't have been involved with at all.'

She was now looking worried, and when I told her it was a school teacher she was devastated. I had established all of these facts in a few seconds without knowing anything about her past.

How did I do this? As this chapter progresses you will understand!

All the detail in my previous book, *Mind Magic*, was laid out to give examples and models for the reader to grasp hold of, understand and use to their advantage. I have focused less on that in this book, opting to show how, with some thought, you can make your mind magic appear to be mind-reading, or a psychological trick.

What I aim to do in this opening chapter is to give you a perspective on psychology in magic, and also some tools to use in magic (and, indeed, in everyday life) that will enhance the experience for your audience and for those you encounter in your day-to-day life. In the coming pages we will look at working with and understanding people, including non-verbal communication and some hard-core psychology that can help you achieve 'miracles' like the one depicted in my story.

THE VALUE OF PSYCHOLOGY IN MAGIC

To begin, I should say that there are as many views on this subject as there are mind magicians. What follows is merely my view, the result of my experience of performing magic for some 30 years.

The use of psychology is fundamental to the success of magical performance. It is a tool that we must use to enhance our act, to throw our audience off the scent, to make them think differently and, most importantly, to make them like us as individuals. Without rapport, you are, at the very best, simply eye candy for your audience; with rapport, however, you are, at least, in touch with your audience.

It is perfectly possible, as you will see in this chapter, to learn techniques that give you some ability to communicate with your audience more effectively, and to help influence their choices and actions. It is virtually impossible, however, to make them act entirely as you wish, especially when you have only just met them. Even a stage hypnotist has to spend the first 20 minutes of his show eliminating the 95 per cent of the audience who cannot be influenced or hypnotized sufficiently.

It is often said that a mind magician should occasionally get something slightly wrong; perhaps a few per cent should be off mark. This enhances the perception that he really is 'reading' your mind in some way, and that he just got one detail wrong. Getting everything spot-on would be just too perfect, implying trickery. This is a view with which I wholeheartedly agree. I can tell you, however, that if you try to rely entirely on psychological methodology, you will get only that few per cent of things right. To meet your audience's expectation that you can

do something they can neither understand nor do for themselves, you simply have to resort to trickery, and for that you need reliable 'magical' methods.

I use psychological techniques all the time when I am performing, to build a rapport with audiences. Even performing at children's birthday parties I use a number of methods to put them at ease and to allay their fears. I am also mindful of my audience's potential state of mind as I construct an act. I certainly do use psychological tools to help pull off tricks, but I know that this can be a gamble. More importantly, I use them as a way of embedding in people's minds that they have seen something special.

FIRST IMPRESSIONS COUNT

Whether you are walking out on stage, meeting a blind date or going for a job interview, in all situations you have to sell yourself, and you have just a few seconds to make the right impression.

Part of the formula for success involves looking the part. If you are performing mind magic, a bright shirt would perhaps seem somewhat incongruous. So give some thought to your appearance and make it fit what your audience might expect. Still more important are the words you might use – the first 10 to 20 words you say will count towards your audience's impression of you. Your task in reciting that first line is to make the audience want to keep listening long enough to hear the second.

'I am going to do some magic!' is not a good line. It is too abrupt and is actually about you – and at this moment your audience does not care about you. You may have already blown it! The first mistake is not greeting and thanking your audience for being there. So a better line might be: 'Good evening. Good to see you here. My name is Marc. Would you like to see something incredible?'

Look at that sentence again and try to break it down. I have greeted them and implicitly thanked them for coming along. I have introduced myself and hooked them in with a question. A question is a great way to build rapport, as it forces your audience to think. As an alternative, a humorous (but polite) one-liner can work equally effectively.

It goes without saying that you should say your opening line with enthusiasm, and certainly with a smile. With the exception of certain types of comedy acts, no performer in any discipline can establish himself without being

upbeat and positive. Once he is 'famous' it may be a different matter – but we have to live with the fact we are working our way up from the bottom.

Another aspect of greeting that is often overlooked is the handshake. I would not expect you to shake everyone's hand if you were working with a big audience, but certainly any helpers or folks in a small group deserve that privilege. Shaking hands with your audience can also be said to establish trust and, most importantly, equality. So offer your hand, making sure it is perfectly vertical. Hold the other person's hand firmly, make eye contact as you shake, and say, 'How do you do?'

KEEPING RAPPORT

Once you have done all this good work to establish yourself, you need to keep the audience interested in you. There is an old saying that goes: 'There is no sweeter sound to any man in any language than the sound of his own name.' Using people's names frequently is a great way of keeping their attention. And doing so also helps us with another problem.

Quite often in your mind magic act you will be working and concentrating on one or two individuals, so how do we keep the rest of the audience engaged? It's easy – talk to them about your helper. There are two forces at play here. Certainly, the remainder of your audience is interested in your helper and how you will be utilizing him or her as an aide. This curiosity stems from a basic human nosiness, and also perhaps from a slightly jealous desire to be the centre of attention themselves. In some cases, it can also be sheer relief that they have not been called up on stage in front of everybody! If your audience is focused on your helper, it naturally follows that, if the helper loses interest, your audience will, too.

To hold the interest of your helpers, you need to be able to do one thing that may sound easy, but actually takes a little bit of practice: you must remember your helpers' names. I am sure we have all been at a party where we have been introduced to someone whose name we have forgotten almost instantly. In fact, you can avoid this problem by remembering the 'Rule of Three'. If you can repeat the person's name three times in reasonably quick succession, it will be firmly embedded in your mind.

Think about how you learn lines from songs, or study for exams. You go over the lines or information repeatedly in your head, or even aloud, and they eventually stick. For example, say you were to say something like, 'I need someone to assist. Would you mind, sir? May I ask your name?', and the audience member replied, 'David.' Should you continue, 'Thank you, sir. What I would like you to do…', you would almost certainly forget his name because you have not repeated it yourself. Better to say something like, 'I need someone to assist. Would you mind, sir? May I ask your name? David? Nice to meet you, David. What I would like you to do, David, is…'. Having repeated his name three times, you have a greater chance of recalling it later.

Another tip for keeping your audience engaged is, obviously, to make sure you talk to them, too. 'David is now going to mix the cards for me…' keeps the audience engaged, as it is directed at them, but it is still focused on your helper. In essence, the secret is to 'wake the audience up' regularly with eye contact and, of course, changes in the pace of your actions and patter. Generally, an audience's attention tends to wane within three or four minutes without additional stimulation. Be aware of this fact, and plan your patter and movements accordingly.

BUILDING CONFIDENCE

Once you have managed to establish some degree of rapport with your audience, your next task is to build their confidence in you. Fortune-tellers often use a technique called 'cold reading' to do this. They make a statement that seems specific to their listener, but is in fact a broad generalization, which nevertheless seems to imply they have gained some intimate knowledge with their subject through mystical means. Combining these standard statements with comments based upon a person's appearance and behaviour can appear to be true mind reading!

This technique of cold reading is sometimes referred to as the 'Barnum effect', after the American showman, P. T. Barnum, who recognized the phenomenon in the fortune-tellers who worked at his circuses. In the 1940s, a well-known psychologist, Bertram Forer, conducted experiments in which collections of these statements were passed off as the results of personality tests. The result was an 85 per cent accuracy rating from his subjects. The types of statements he used are summarized in the table opposite, which also shows in

Barnum/Forer-type statement	Rational explanation
You have a need for others to like you.	This basic human need speaks for itself.
You tend to be critical of yourself.	This is driven by the need for 'survival', for self-monitoring and improvement.
You can be extroverted, outgoing and sociable, while at times you can be quite introverted.	This line works for us all, even though the balance varies.
Disciplined and in control on the outside, you tend to be insecure internally.	A replaying of the previous line that looks different and builds the illusion.
You feel you have some personality weaknesses, but you feel able to work around them.	We all know we are not perfect, but we aspire to be. We think we are better than others!
You prefer a certain amount of change and are frustrated when restricted and held back.	A truism! Who wouldn't be frustrated if held back?
Your faith in others is sometimes misplaced.	We have all been let down in the past...
You feel you are an independent thinker and do not accept facts from others without proof.	... and so we tend to think our model of the world is best and need persuading otherwise.
You have found it unwise to be too open in revealing your inner thoughts.	Yes, you have been let down and so you are naturally wary.
At times you have had serious doubts as to the decisions you have made.	Again, a truism. We all wonder 'what if?'
Some of your dreams and hopes tend to be unrealistic.	Natural self-doubt. When we don't get what we desire, we grow angry and frustrated.
You have potential and abilities that you have not fully exploited.	Again, it's human nature to wish for more than we have.

relatively simple terms why most of us would tend to agree with assertions such as these.

Mind magicians might use this powerful tool for a slightly different purpose than that of fortune-tellers. They still need to build confidence, but the objective is not to prove that they can tell fortunes. Every successful mind magician has to establish that he or she is a great 'people person' who can interpret a person's inner thoughts and feelings from the series of external clues and signals they give off. Rather than make many such remarks in quick succession, they might simply seed their patter with just one or two examples. Just like a fortune-teller, however, they might also interpret other signs and signals from the people with whom they are talking that give away even more detail. The way they dress, their posture, their various facial expressions and so on are all useful extra titbits of information we can use to build up a picture.

In essence, weaving general statements into your patter is a way of fishing for reactions. Any such statement hardly ever misses completely – so you are always at least correct in part. But from time to time you will get a major reaction and know you have hit target. For example, during your conversation with someone you might remark, 'I get the feeling that you are nervous and insecure around people you do not know well.' That sounds specific on the surface, but is in fact true of pretty much all of us, even hard-bitten entertainers like me. Yet they are likely to nod in agreement and move their body closer to yours as a sign that you have touched on something. Then it is your time to prepare for a revelation of your own from a force or some other trickery.

Saying something that is undoubtedly true and relevant, without the benefit of any apparent prior knowledge, has the effect of building confidence and makes other assertions and predictions seem stronger. There are many other examples of such generalized statements published in books and on websites. I suggest you do some research, and I have no doubt you will be able to come up with your own interpretations and fresh ideas.

For example, you could talk about 'an incident from when you were a child involving water or some liquid…' (see Extra Scentsory Perception, pages 30-4). It is an almost surefire bet that as a child, the audience member had an incident with liquid. He or she may have nearly drowned in a swimming pool, or he or she may have been punished for spilling some water. I'm sure you get the picture.

NON-VERBAL COMMUNICATION

Did you know that when we speak, only seven per cent of what we attempt to communicate to people is imparted through the words we use? About 38 per cent is communicated through the way we speak, the tone of our voice and so on. But by far the majority of our message, some 55 per cent, is given through non-verbal communication.

We are all familiar with the term 'body language', used to describe the science of interpreting posture, gestures and facial expressions, in order to gauge how people feel about themselves, their world and you. This is a complex and detailed subject, and I do not intend to go too far into it in this book – although I do recommend it as a very useful tool for both life and magic. But the lesson we can learn from the concept of body language is simple and very powerful: *If we have a rapport with someone, we can obtain more information from them.*

Having taught you a little bit about how to gain and build rapport, I now want to take you to the next level...

A NEW SCIENCE

During the 1970s, Richard Bandler, a psychologist, and John Grinder, a professor of linguistics, began to explore the relationship between our thoughts, speech and actions, and how this relationship leads us to certain patterns of behaviour, and to give certain responses. Over time, with the help of workers in other fields, they developed the science of NLP, or neuro-linguistic programming. In short, NLP examines how our mental organization is affected by language (used by us and those around us) and in turn affects the way we programme ourselves to behave.

NLP is primarily used as a self-improvement tool. The theory is that, if you understand how your thoughts and behaviour are programmed by your inter-pretation of information, it could be possible to adjust that programming by learning different ways of seeing the information you receive. I'll give you an example, one which I was using long before I even knew NLP existed.

A lot of people, especially children, are frightened of balloons. They are, of course, scared of them bursting with a loud bang! Such people associate balloons with fear. If, however, you were to suggest that if a balloon should burst, they must point at you and shout, 'Neener, neener!' then the programming has been dramatically changed. Now the association is with fun – taking the mickey out of someone. Now they actively want that balloon to burst!

The study of NLP is most fascinating, and I thoroughly recommend it to anyone. For the mind magician in particular, there is one aspect of NLP that is a powerful tool in terms of building even greater rapport with the audience, and interpreting a person's inner processes.

Communication Style and Representational Systems

We all process information in different ways. Some of us are more practical and hands-on, while others are great thinkers and have creative minds. NLP defines five representational systems based upon our five senses, to categorize how we individually process information internally. They are:

- Visual   Linked with sight and vision
- Auditory   Linked with sounds and speech
- Kinaesthetic Linked with feeling and emotion
- Gustatory   Linked to taste
- Olfactory   Linked to smell

It is very important to remember that we all process all kinds of information all the time. But we do typically have a preference for one or another of the styles. The importance of knowing this is that if we know how our internal process is biased, we can be more active in adapting and changing our programming through the use of more targeted language and stimuli. Even more interesting is that, if we can establish someone else's style and adapt our language accordingly, we have a better chance of influencing or convincing them in an argument.

For example, if we are trying to persuade someone to accept our point of view, we might say, 'Can you see what I mean?' That will work well for a visual person, but not so well for an auditory person, who might prefer to be asked, 'Do you hear what I am saying?' Simply put, we humans act tend to take the path of least resistance. If we can remove or lower barriers through our choice of words, we would smooth the way for what we wish to achieve.

In reality, most people are predominantly visual, fewer are auditory and still fewer are kinaesthetic. A minority are gustatory or olfactory. We will focus on the most predominant styles: visual, auditory and kinaesthetic.

The Eyes Have It

It is said that the eyes are the windows to the soul, and as far as NLP is concerned, that is indeed the case. By observing people's eye movements when processing information, we can see some clues as to their dominant representational system. Consider the diagram below, which represents the face of a hypothetical person we may be working with, as if we were looking straight at them (thus their left would be to your right). If you ask a person a question which requires them to access and process buried information, their eyes will tend to look towards the zone of their dominant style.

Zone 1 is Visualistic
Zone 2 is Auditory
Zone 3 is Kinaesthetic

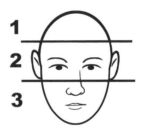

A great question to ask is, 'Who was your favourite teacher at primary school?' This information is usually buried deeply, and the person will have to search for it. Visual people will tend to 'look' for the memory. They will actually see an image of that person in their mind's eye, and will tend to look upwards as they visualize the person. You can attempt to confirm this once they have answered the question; use a probing statement such as 'So could you see a picture of Miss Johnson in your mind?' Auditory people will tend to look to the side, towards their ears as if they are hearing that person speak to them. You could confirm this with a statement such as 'I expect you could hear Miss Johnson speaking to you above the noise of the classroom.' Kinaesthetic people will look down when accessing information. They 'feel' their memories, and you could confirm this by saying, 'I expect you recall how nice Miss Johnson was and all the great times you had in class.'

Ask the Right Questions

Knowing the right questions to ask – and what to do when you don't get a clear response – is important to understand. Good questions are ones that make the person think deeply. If the answer is relatively fresh in their mind, their movements are likely to be less definite, and will almost certainly be more brief.

Some good questions to ask are:

- Who was your favourite teacher at primary school?
  (Make sure you specify the school.)
- What was your first pet's name?
- When you were seven years old, what kind of car did your father drive?
- When you were six years old, what did you want for Christmas?
- What was your favourite birthday present as a child?
- Who was your best friend at secondary school?
- Who was your first boyfriend/girlfriend?
- What colour was your front door when you were nine years old?

You can, of course, come up with your own additional questions. Remember, however, that there are two golden rules for any questions that you may decide to ask:

1. Do not ask further questions about the same subject. (If you ask several questions about school, then everyone present will be thinking about their school days, and the memories will be less deep as a result.)

2. Do not add a preamble to your question, such as 'I want you to go back to the time when you were seven years old and to think of your days in school.' (Again, the person's memory will be too much to the fore, and this will skew your results.)

If you do not get a clear response, ask another question about a different subject. If you still don't get a clear response, then you should move on to another person. Ultimately it does not matter if you can't gauge everyone, or indeed, anyone at all. This is just an extra finesse for your act.

Delving Deeper

Take a look at the more detailed depiction of our subject's face below. You see we now have two parts to our visualistic, auditory and kinaesthetic zones. This is where the power of using this subset of NLP really lies.

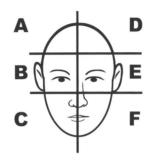

You now have a way of determining whether your subject is actually recalling a memory, or making something up as they go along. Simply put, if the eyes go up to Zone D (their left, your right), it is a memory. If they go up to Zone A (their right), they are working to make something up! Also, take note of the lower right position Zone F. This indicates an internal dialogue or conflict. You may have touched upon a raw nerve, or they are uncertain about what to reveal to you, whereas movement to Zone C implies a simpler emotional response. If their response flits between Zones B and E, they are most likely simply showing they are Auditory. If they linger too long on Zone B, they may be making something up.

Do not, however, assume that someone is lying if they look up and to their right. It is essential to gain experience with people in general and with each subject in particular. We all use a mixture of the styles all the time, and on one particular day, depending upon how he or she feels inside, your subject may give a confusing result. Learn to watch people to see how they react, so you can gauge their normal behaviour as a comparison to how they react when questioned. Use this knowledge wisely and carefully.

Using NLP

Without resorting to studying NLP in depth, there are three main ways to utilise it in your life – and in your mind magic.

1. Use of Language

In talking to your subjects, learn the key types of words each representational style prefers to hear. Some examples are:

Visualistic   Look, see, view, light, focus, imagine, perspective, etc.
Auditory   Say, hear, remark, listen, talk, discuss, loud, etc.
Kinaesthetic   Touch, grasp, feel, hold, heavy, soft, etc.

Buy a book on NLP and you will find much more useful information to help you become more adept at these skills.

2. As an 'Apparent' Method

If you take some time to explain to your audience the basics of NLP and how it helps you to interpret their responses, they will most definitely be intrigued.

For example, look at the audience while you ask questions about their chosen playing card, and ask them to always answer 'yes' loudly in their minds to any question about the card. Ask then about the card's colour, suit and number, then announce the chosen card. The implication is that you have correctly ascertained their chosen card by watching their eye responses (which would, of course, move to the construction zone when they are having to 'lie' with their answer). But the simple reality is that you forced the card. This apparent mastery of psychology is, to many audiences, no less amazing than a sleight of hand or any other magician's skill.

This is a similar approach to that which we will use in the Stimuleye mind trick (see page 25-9). However, be sure not to make the same mistake as one stage mind-reader I saw recently. He announced that he would tell which cards his helpers were holding using NLP, and explained how he would be looking for their eye responses to guide him. He then began to ask questions, but dipped his head and placed his hand on his forehead (as in the style of the old-fashioned mind-reader). There was no way he could have been reading their eye movements – he wasn't even looking at their faces! I heard a few members of the audience comment on this faux pas during the interval.

The bottom line is to be consistent. If you are going to imply that you will be using psychological methods when performing the trick in question, make it look as if you are doing so!

3. As a Means for Miracles

Ultimately, if you do discuss these topics with your audience, they will tend to find you more engaging and memorable. That is the most powerful aspect, in my opinion, of working with a tool such as NLP. Quite simply, it is an interesting tool, and people want to know more about it. You have proven yourself to have many talents as a performer and, because you will tell people more about themselves, you have given them something special.

But real miracles do occur from time to time, as in the story I told at the opening of this chapter (see page 10). On that day I guess I was lucky and made the right connections, but I also used a bit of NLP. When I asked about the subject's first boyfriend, her eyes followed a very unusual pattern, which I interpreted in the following ways:

- They went up to Zone D, the memory zone – she saw her first love.
- They went to Zone C, the emotion zone – showing deep affection for the person whom she was recalling.
- They went and lingered at Zone F, the conflict zone – showing concern and confusion.
- They went to Zone A, the construction zone – she told me a 'lie' about who it was.
- They went back to the conflict zone – she felt bad about lying to me.

I felt confident enough about the general cause of her conflict to make some lucky guesses and I was spot-on – I really did scare myself with that one! One note of caution: I urge you not to try anything like that with anyone until you are well practised. Even more importantly, never ask a person deeply personal questions in front of anyone else. You'll recall from my story that before I delved into the true answer to my question, I took my subject to one side, to save her embarrassment.

However you choose to use psychology in your magic – simply as misdirection, as a spoof method or just as a convincer – use it wisely. All the disciplines of psychology combined do not give a single robust method of performing miracles. From time to time, this method will make you look like a star, but more often than not you will be largely reliant upon your basic skills as a mind magician for a successful performance.

CHAPTER 2:
THE SIGNS ARE THERE

Psychologists tell us that we should not regard the human body and mind as separate entities. Rather, they comprise a 'whole': a unique machine with many components interacting in a myriad of complex ways, each part constantly affecting all others as we plod though our daily existence. I am very sure this is true, although without a formal qualification in psychology it might be difficult for me to prove, and so all I can relate is my own experience.

When I am not performing or writing about magic, I teach business people how to communicate more effectively with their colleagues and clients. As we have learned in the previous chapter, only a small percentage of what we have to say is actually related through the words we choose. Much more of what we are trying to communicate is hidden in the way we use and speak those words. By far the greater part – around 60 per cent of our message – is entirely non-verbal. Our gestures, stance, eye movements, twitches and even the odours we emit speak volumes about our state of mind, our feelings about those to whom we are speaking, our inner emotions and our sincerity.

Utilizing this non-verbal communication can prove a wonderful tool in your daily life, as it can help you to understand people and their reactions to you more effectively. But it is a difficult subject to learn. I do not profess to be an absolute expert in the area, but I do know enough to be able to use it to enhance my magical perform-ances. So, as an example of how to utilize these techniques, let's use a little trickery to imply that we have a unique ability to interpret minute physiological signals to our advantage.

Here are three effects that do just that. They are presented as one programme, but could just as effectively be presented individually or along with other effects.

STIMULEYE

As mentioned earlier, the eyes are said to be the windows to the soul, and in my life experience I have found this to be absolutely true. Even if we do not understand the psychology in great depth, we can easily tell when someone is happy, sad or distressed, for example, by the look in their eyes.

Earlier in the book I discussed some techniques which really do use some hard psychology that you can use as a bit of fun and to enhance your 'mind magic'. Here we will simply add a psychological twist to enhance a straightforward trick.

◎ ◎ ◎ You Will Need ◎ ◎ ◎
- Three helpers
- A pack of playing cards (with a little bit of preparation)

◎ ◎ ◎ The Trick ◎ ◎ ◎

You have three volunteers whom you have never met before: Tony, Jo and Kathy.

'We as humans typically believe that we can keep our inner thoughts to ourselves. We are very much mistaken!', you say.

'People are not made up of little bits and pieces simply thrown together haphazardly. We are complex machines, and all of our components – body, mind and soul – work together. To me, this means your body is a beacon that can show me your inner thoughts.'

Shuffle a pack of cards and have Kathy and Jo take one each. Tony will also take a card, but in a somewhat different manner.

'Tony, I will spread the cards in front of you. I want you to touch the back of one card, thank you. Now it is important for this experiment that no one, especially me and you, knows which card you have chosen at this point.'

Carefully instruct him to remove the card, but *without* turning it over so he can see its face. Instead, turn the whole pack over yourself and have Tony insert his card into the deck so that it is back to front from the rest.

'Now we know no one can see the card you have chosen, but we can be certain which card it is when we look through the cards later.'

Put the cards in their box and hand them to one of your helpers.

'I am going to try to interpret some of your unconscious signals and messages. It is absolutely essential that you give me no verbal clues at all. Keep very quiet until I finally ask you if I am correct.

'I will talk to each of you in turn and I will name several things in quick succession. They will be an apparently random succession of words, numbers, names of cards, suits and so on. It will most likely seem meaningless to you, but whenever I say a word that fits your card, or in some way correctly describes it, I want you to say a very loud YES. But please be very clear: only say that word in your mind. Do not say it aloud.'

With your helpers standing in front of you, turn to Jo and say, 'Red, blue, green, five, six, ten, queen, spade, four, jack, diamond, ace, club, heart, picture, seven, king …'

Stop and turn to Kathy. 'I am getting a bit distracted here. I did say I would deal with you in turn, but, Kathy, I can hear your mind much louder than Jo here. Your card is the six of spades, isn't it?' She nods in astonishment and you turn back to Jo and say a few more words, but faster this time. 'Two, four, club, diamond, heart, diamond. The four of diamonds. That's right, isn't it?' She nods in even more astonishment.

'You see, I was looking for responses from you that you thought you could hide, but by watching for a slight flicker in the eye or twitch of the nose I can tell when you made that association with the words I spoke.

'What is even more incredible is that we can often sense things we have not seen, such as your card, Tony. Perhaps it is because you can see the most subtle print marks from the back, or maybe you saw a card or two as I shuffled them, but you have a card in your mind. It may be in the very back of your mind, but it is there nonetheless. I will now try to get your card.'

Face Tony and speak another stream of words: 'Two, four, club, nine, queen, spade, four, jack, diamond, spot, joker, ace, club, heart … the nine of hearts, correct?'

Of course, Tony cannot answer your question, as even he does not know the card he has chosen.

Ask to be handed the pack of cards again. Take them out of the box and begin to slowly spread through them until you find the card that Tony turned upside down at the very beginning. It is indeed the nine of hearts.

◎ ◎ ◎ The Secret ◎ ◎ ◎

The opening trick of *Mind Magic*, my previous book, was called Predictable Behaviour. In that trick you predicted which card someone might choose; this was achieved through 'forcing' a card. (This is where people think that their choice of card is random and entirely free of outside influence, but they have, in fact, made their decision entirely under your control.) You are easily able to apparently 'predict' it because you have pre-determined the card.

This trick is not a prediction; it is a divination. To be more precise, it is a triple divination. What's more, rather than simply 'predicting thoughts', as you might have done with the trick in *Mind Magic*, here you are apparently using psychological responses to gain the information you need. Of course, the real manner in which you get the information is far simpler. It is actually achieved through forcing the cards, only on this occasion we use two different forcing techniques. We also employ what is perhaps the most useful technique in magic – time misdirection. This means throwing your audience off the scent by causing their memories to be distorted simply by adding a time delay.

To prepare for this trick, choose your force cards. They can be any three cards you like, but try to have a variety of suits and numbers; do not choose all fours, for example. Place the first two force cards on top of the deck. Place the last force card – in our case, the nine of hearts – in the deck about 17 to 20 cards from the top. Make sure to place it upside down to the rest of the pack.

The only other thing you need to learn to do is a false shuffle. This is an apparently normal shuffling of the pack that keeps at least part of the deck or the whole deck in the same order (see box on page 28).

While you are talking about psychology, casually give the cards a (false) shuffle. Explain that each of your helpers needs a card, and take the following actions and say the following words:

'You each need a card. Let me just finish shuffling.'

Take the top card and give it to your first helper.

'Here, you take this one and…'

Shuffle some more.

'Here, you take this one,' you continue, handing the next card to your second helper as you do so.

False Shuffle

The basic idea behind a false shuffle is that you apparently shuffle the cards into a random order, but in reality you secretly keep them in order. Many variations exist, but here is a simple false shuffle that will suit the various tricks in this book.

Hold the deck in your right hand with the faces of the cards upwards. With your left thumb, draw off three cards and let them fall into the left hand. Then, whilst continuing the same motion, drop the remainder of the deck onto the three cards in your left hand. Take the deck back into the right hand and repeat the process, this time counting off four cards and, again, dropping the deck onto them.

Now pause for a second and casually turn the whole deck over while passing it from the left hand to the right. The deck will now have its back facing towards you. Count off three cards just as before, dropping the deck onto them. Then repeat with four cards just as you did previously. What you have done is to move seven cards from the front to the back of the deck and then immediately return them to their original places.

You may think that what you have done will be obvious to your audience, but if you follow two golden rules it will not be. First, always look at your audience while you are shuffling. Never look at the cards. Practise until you can do this confidently. Second, never say 'I am shuffling the cards', as this will call attention to them. Just shuffle and people will simply remember that you shuffled the deck!

Shuffle some more, as you turn to the third helper and say, 'And you will choose your card in a different manner.'

As described above, spread the cards with their backs upwards in front of your helpers, but make sure you keep the first third of the deck together. The face-up card is hidden here and we don't want that to be seen just yet.

Have your third helper take a card out of the deck, and make sure it stays facing down and unseen. Close the deck, turn it upside down and lift off about 15 cards or so. Have each helper place his or her chosen card onto the deck. Replace the 15 cards on top of these cards, pop the whole deck into the box and you are all set.

From here, the trick is relatively simple. Just say the various words – it matters little which words you use, as long as they relate to cards. Thus, you may mention numbers, suits, colours and so on, in any order you like. The one thing you must do, of course, is to mention all the words that describe your three force cards. If you were actually interpreting your helpers'

reactions, then naturally they would need to hear you say the right words!

Once you have named the first two cards, turn to your third helper and say a few more words before naming the final force card. Next, remove the cards from the box and carefully spread through them. There are, of course, two cards reversed in the deck: our force card and the card your third helper randomly chose. If you spread through from the top of the deck you will find the force card first. Remove it and take your applause.

Put the deck away and no one will be any the wiser about the odd card still lying round the wrong way in the pack!

◎ ◎ ◎ Final Thoughts ◎ ◎ ◎

Time misdirection and the correct choice of words and actions are what make this trick work. If you were simply to say, 'Here, look, I am shuffling. Here, choose a card,' then blatantly hand your helpers the top card, your audience could rightfully challenge you. The secret is to lure them into a memory trap.

If you use the flow of words given above, your audience will recall that your helper was told he or she would get a card from a shuffled deck. Surely that must be random – mustn't it? But the real mental trick we play on the helpers involves giving the last helper what appears to be a truly free choice. When they think back and replay the sequence of events in their minds, they will all very likely believe they were given a free choice, simply because the events in this trick happen in quick succession, and it's difficult to know the significance of any single event until well after it has occurred.

EXTRA SCENTSORY PERCEPTION

Many people are aware of 'body language', and will quite often remark on another person's posture or gestures, thinking they know what their thoughts or feelings are. Furthermore, as most of you know, animals, including humans, often communicate by smell. We even attract our sexual partners this way using pheromones. The changes in our body odour are usually too subtle and gradual to be of any practical entertainment value, however, and so we have to resort to some trickery to make it look possible!

Here is another example of how we can turn a basic mind trick into what seems like a true psychological effect.

◉ ◉ ◉ You Will Need ◉ ◉ ◉

- Three helpers
- Three identical pens or pencils
- Three unused perfume sample cards (like the ones you sniff to try out different fragrances in the shops)
- A bottle of perfume or aftershave – the cheaper and nastier the better!

◉ ◉ ◉ The Trick ◉ ◉ ◉

Tony, Kathy and Jo are still with you and want to see more magic. You point out to them a bottle of cheap perfume that is sitting on a table to one side.

'Interpreting human eye signals about current situations is relatively simple, but there are other more challenging tests we could try. Psychologists tell us that even distant memories of strong emotions such as great pleasure or extreme fear can invoke a strong reaction in us today. Even though we might think we have that memory compartmentalized and under control, it can actually affect us at a physiological level without us even realizing. Let me show you an example.'

Hand each of your helpers a perfume card and a pen, take a few steps away and turn your back on them.

'I have turned away as I do not want to receive any explicit or obvious visual clues from what I am about to ask you to do. Nor do I want to be accused of reading your pen movements so I can tell which card belongs to whom.

'Listen carefully to what I have to say before you draw or write anything. In a moment, I will count down from five to zero, and in that time I want you to try to recall a strong memory from your childhood. It may be a bad memory, such as a time when you were frightened or hurt in some way, or it may be something a little more positive.

'When I get to zero, I would like you to capture one simple image that in some way sums up the experience and make a small sketch on the card you are holding. Don't make it too complicated – a simple line drawing will be perfect.'

Count down and allow them a few moments to draw on their cards.

'Have you all done that, yes? Now I want you all to hold your card between your palms, as if you are praying. Concentrate on the memory again. Try to reconnect with the emotions you experienced at the time.'

Pause here for some 15 or 20 seconds.

'I want one of you to collect all three cards together and mix them up so I don't know their order, and I want you to spray each card with the perfume. Make sure you give them all a good soaking, then lay the cards down on the table.'

Turn around and pick up the cards. Begin to examine the pictures drawn on them. They are a house, a cat and some wavy lines.

Spend the next minute or so gently wafting each card in turn under your nose. Occasionally look at your individual helpers inquisitively. You even walk up to Tony and waft some air from his body towards your nose.

'I think I have it all now. But I need a little help from you, Tony. You drew the house, right?' He nods in amazement – your first success.

'This is odd. I could detect your odour on the card through the perfume, but I can't definitely tell if this is a good or bad memory. It's a good memory, isn't it!' He nods again.

'Is this a place that you visited

regularly, like your grandmother's or an uncle's house?' He nods some more; you move on.

Taking the 'cat' card in your hand, approach Jo. 'Now, this could get a little predictable. If I work out which of these two cards is yours, then I suppose it makes me finding Kathy's card somewhat of an anticlimax, so I have to go for broke.

'Hmmm, I think, Jo, you recalled a really bad experience when you were a child, is that right?' She acknowledges you are correct. 'This was a situation where you nearly drowned or perhaps got caught by the tide when swimming or something like that, am I right? You see, I could smell the fear on your card.' She confirms with a nod as you turn to Kathy. 'And, boy, could I smell the love for your cat!'

Your helpers are already impressed, but they are even more astounded when you add "Oh, and thanks, Jo, for spraying the cards when I wasn't looking.'

How did you know that?

◎ ◎ ◎ The Secret ◎ ◎ ◎

This effect has two key secrets. The first is so simple it seems almost a crime, but it is, in fact, a proven technique. If you have read my previous book, *Mind Magic*, you will recall a trick called Whose Life Is It, Anyway? The method here is very similar, but in this case the perfumed cards are all marked with very light pencil dots. Mark one card with a single dot, one with two dots and the last card with three dots. Simply hand out the cards in order so that you later know whose is whose. It doesn't matter how thoroughly they are mixed up; you will always know which one belongs to which person.

So you already have the first part of the effect in place. You aren't really interpreting the subtleties of your helpers' body odours; you don't need to because you have marked the cards! The second secret is even simpler. It is a dose of good old BULL! What you are doing is trying to envisage the situation from the picture to try to second-guess what that particular person's experience was.

When you perform this with real people, you will have no idea what they will imagine and what they will actually draw. Most will tend to go with a positive memory – that is only natural. A few will go for something negative; it is certainly better 'theatrically' if at least one of your three chooses a bad memory, but not essential. This is why the negative was given more emphasis in the patter.

Determining whether a picture is 'positive' or 'negative' is not an exact science; it is open to interpretation. In fact, if you get this wrong for one or two people, it does not matter a great deal when you can correctly establish who drew which image. There are some images that are fairly obvious. Domestic animals, hearts, the sun and so on – all these are very positive. Weapons, wild animals and so on might be easily recognized as negative. Some are less easy to tell straight away. A house such as in our example could be a place of good memories, of holidays and loving relations, or it could be a source of painful reminders of isolation.

The simplest tip I can offer is to look at each picture and see what memories and associations it evokes for you and work from there. For example, you may see a flower, which is more likely to be positive. You could say to your helper: 'Tony, you drew the flower, correct? Now, this is a positive experience, I think,' slightly raising the tone of your voice in a kind of 'questioning' manner.

This is a very useful technique as, if you are correct, you can take credit for being spot on. If it is not correct, then it doesn't matter. Why? Because you were clearly asking a question and not stating a hard fact. Essentially, act as if you were not claiming that question to be part of your magic. This is an approach you can use often in your mind magic.

Once you have established the memory, however, you can then say something along the lines of, 'I thought I could detect the anxiety in your odour, but, no, you are right – it is something much more positive.'

The key lesson is that, even if your thoughts on the experiences them-selves were wrong, your bottom line is that you correctly established which card belonged to whom.

◎ ◎ ◎ Final Thoughts ◎ ◎ ◎

You can find references to people's choice of images in books on psychology, which may help you with an effect such as this one. But my advice is not to be too reliant upon hard evidence. The really good mind magician learns to work with the audience he has, and to take his lead from it. This skill can take time to build, but it is perhaps the most useful one you can learn.

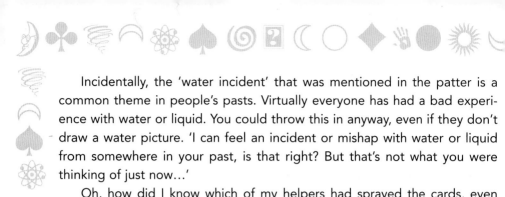

Incidentally, the 'water incident' that was mentioned in the patter is a common theme in people's pasts. Virtually everyone has had a bad experience with water or liquid. You could throw this in anyway, even if they don't draw a water picture. 'I can feel an incident or mishap with water or liquid from somewhere in your past, is that right? But that's not what you were thinking of just now...'

Oh, how did I know which of my helpers had sprayed the cards, even though I was not watching? Simple. There are three clues you could look for. First, the person may be the only one not holding his or her pen (he or she might have put it away to free up his or her hands), whereas the others might still be holding theirs. Or, the person may have spilled or sprayed some perfume on his or her hands, and would therefore be wringing or wiping them. But most obviously, he or she will likely smell of the perfume on his or her body! Hence, be sure to pick the cheapest and nastiest one you can find.

THAT ESPECIAL SOMETHING

Having great magical powers is wonderful, even if they are just tricks. But power becomes even stronger when you 'give it away'. Having seen you give two demonstrations of your ability to sense the subtle changes in other people's minds and bodies, wouldn't it be even more wonderful to help somebody else develop their empathic skills? To close this chapter, we not only change the style of effect, but we also shift the power right into the hands – and the minds – of your spectators.

◎ ◎ ◎ You Will Need ◎ ◎ ◎

- A helper
- An envelope containing a letter (more of which later)
- An old wedding or engagement ring
- An old coin (the browner the better)
- A photograph of an elderly lady

◎ ◎ ◎ The Trick ◎ ◎ ◎

Kathy, Tony and Jo are still with you. Turn your attention to Kathy.

'You had the clearest signals of all earlier, and I thank you for that, as it makes my job a little easier. But you know this is just a skill – a skill we can all learn and develop. I can show you how right now, if you are willing to learn.

'The signals and messages I received from you all earlier were quite indistinct and subtle, but then I am very experienced. To help you, may I suggest an experiment with a much stronger emotion.'

Remove an old envelope from a pocket and take out the contents: an old coin, an engagement ring and a photograph of an elderly lady.

'This is my grandmother. Her name is Florence, and she has been dead some 15 or 16 years now. When we cleared out her home we found this envelope that was addressed to me, and in it were these things. She wanted me to have them, but one of them in particular has a very special significance to me.

'I wonder if you can tell from my subconscious responses which of them it is. Here is what I suggest you do. I want you to ask me three questions in

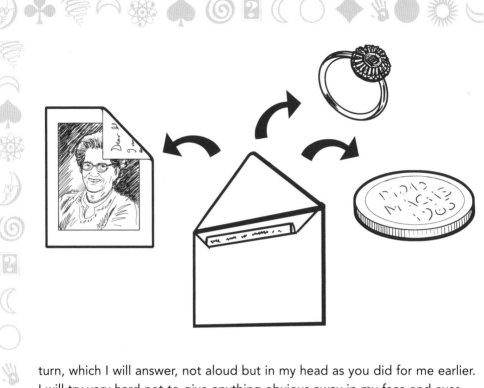

turn, which I will answer, not aloud but in my head as you did for me earlier. I will try very hard not to give anything obvious away in my face and eyes.

'The three questions are: Is the coin the special item? Is the photo the special item? Is the ring the special item?'

Take a deep breath and sit down. Kathy asks the questions, but seems unsure, so you suggest she asks again, which she does. After several moments of consideration she announces that she thinks it is the ring.

'That is interesting. I wonder if you are correct. There is something else I didn't show you in the envelope.'

Take out a hand-written letter, hand it to Tony and have him read it aloud.

'My dear grandchild, as you know my health is not as good as it used to be. As I lay in my bed I think back on all those precious memories, including the long summers when you would come to stay with me. You used to ask me nearly every day to tell you the story of my lucky ring; the ring that your grandfather bought me when we became engaged – the one that brought me such a happy and fulfilled life. I recall that when you were perhaps seven or eight I said that I would give you this ring someday because I wanted you to enjoy the same kind of luck that I did. And so when I do pass on I want to keep my promise and leave this ring in your care, in fond memory of my life past and yours to come. Much love – Grandma.'

Clearly Kathy was correct, and is now just a little tearful. You have not only shared your power, but also made a deep connection.

◎ ◎ ◎ The Secret ◎ ◎ ◎

I wonder if you have guessed the secret involved here. Is it another force? No, it is not. In fact, any one of the three objects could have been chosen. The principle involved is that of a 'multiple out'. This means that because your audience does not know the outcome of the effect, you have the opportunity to direct the presentation differently depending upon the helper's choice. (See page 43 for more on 'multiple outs'.)

To prepare, find the items you need. First, you need the photograph. Perhaps download an image from the Internet, but try to make it look old using photo software. On the back of the photograph, write a short note that is apparently from your grandmother. It should read something like:

To my darling grandson, I hope this picture will act as a reminder of our special times together – much love, Grandma x

Track down some old writing paper. You will probably find an old pad in your drawer or gathering dust at your local post office. Write the letter out, changing it to make it more personal to you. Perhaps an elderly relative could write it for you for more realism.

Find an old ring and an old coin, or perhaps a medallion. Do nothing with the ring, but pop into your local engravers and ask them to engrave a short message on the coin, something like:

A special wish – Grandma

Fold the letter so that it can remain in the envelope unseen. Perhaps use a larger envelope than you might usually use for this type of paper, and fold the letter just once. Write 'To Marc', or whatever your name is, on the front of the envelope, pop everything in the envelope and you are all set.

Lay the objects out on the table, ensuring the reverse sides of the photo and coin are facing downwards. Have your helper ask the questions and proceed as follows.

If they name the ring, then dip into the envelope, remove the letter and have somebody read it aloud. This is the perfect (and most likely) outcome, as there is a separate prediction in the form of the letter. As the letter is being read, you may wish to casually pick up the coin and photo, and pop them into the envelope, which goes back into your pocket.

If the photo is chosen, push it towards your helper and say, 'There is a message on the photo which I think will confirm whether you are correct or not.' They will naturally pick it up look it over and read the message. Again, while this is happening, you can slip the ring and coin into your pocket.

The least strong outcome could be the choice of the coin; however, with a few carefully chosen words, you can actually add to the effect. If your helper names the coin, it is not powerful enough to simply turn it over and show the inscription. Try this instead.

'Have you ever had a lucky charm? Something special given to you by someone you love? I was given this coin by Grandma on my fifth birthday. When I opened the package I was disappointed to see just a penny as my birthday gift, but she asked me to turn it over and read the inscription...' Ask your helper to turn over the coin. 'Then I had to close my eyes, wish for what I really wanted and count to ten. When I opened my eyes what I really wanted was there – a brand-new bike.'

Of course, while you were telling the story you put the ring and photo away in the envelope, and your helpers are left in no doubt that the penny was indeed the special item!

◎ ◎ ◎ Final Thoughts ◎ ◎ ◎

The ability to know where and when to perform any magic trick is an essential skill that any magician needs to learn. Common sense applies, but experience will help you immensely as well. A trick such as this one is certainly not an 'opener' that you would use to start your show. This kind of trick will prove much more effective when done at the conclusion of a set of tricks, when you have already established your credibility. This is not least for the reason that it is in some ways an obvious method. Performing it carefully helps to avoid that connection being made. But if you have proven your ability to read the signs, then why shouldn't anyone else be able to do it?

What is really great about magic – almost all kinds of magic, actually – is that you can take one idea and make it work in dozens of ways. In fact, there are only about nine different tricks in the world. If you are smart enough, you can show those dozens of things to the same audience over and over again and they won't be any the wiser.

If you are familiar with the original tricks that inspired those we have covered in this chapter, I hope that you will now have a good idea of how you can twist presentations around to suit the style of your act and the persona you wish to create. If you have no previous experience on which to base a comparison, I recommend you read as many books and look at as many DVDs as you can in order to start appreciating how just a simple adjustment to your style and method can make all the difference.

CHAPTER 3:
UNDER THE INFLUENCE

I consider myself to be a free-thinking man with strict morals, yet I still find myself making decisions and choices I do not feel totally in control of. While sometimes my conscience wins and I get my way, the majority of the time I find that my mind is influenced by some external force or another. This affects some of the most crucial decisions I have to make from day to day, such as 'Which breakfast cereal should I buy?', or even 'Should I have red or brown sauce on my fish and chips?'

Yes, I will admit to being slightly flippant, but the power of advertising can be literally overwhelming. And the most pernicious forms of advertising work at a subconscious level, not simply informing us of our choices and options, but actually creating desire and moral arguments as to why we should choose one product (be it a hamburger or a political party) over the other.

We are, as a species, easily led. We typically don't like to make decisions for ourselves, even if we outwardly say we do – and that makes us easy to influence and manipulate. Our saving grace is that the majority of us accept our inane gullibility and are happy to let ourselves be guided by others.

Magicians of all kinds frequently use this natural compliance to facilitate their magical methods. The reach of influence is far wider than just advertising and magic, and so in this chapter we are going to explore how we can take the concept of 'influence' and give a demonstration of human gullibility, creating a little mind magic as we go along.

CHOCOHOLIC

We all know that we are constantly bombarded with advertising. The advertising industry likes to categorize us into segments based upon where we live, our social status, our gender, and so on, in order to focus their efforts more effectively. If we understand that premise, then would it not be possible, given that we can learn a few facts about a person, to predict the product choices they are most likely to make?

In this next trick we will use a little mind magic to give the impression that our helpers are not just an 'open book', but are also very easily led!

◎ ◎ ◎ You Will Need ◎ ◎ ◎
- Three helpers
- A notebook
- Some pre-prepared cards (about postcard size)
- Three different chocolate bars

◎ ◎ ◎ The Trick ◎ ◎ ◎

You are joined around the table by three new acquaintances: Jon, Michelle and Sandra.

'While we think we are relatively free-thinking people, we are all in fact the products of a lifetime of influences. Our parents and teachers, family and friends, have all affected who we are and the way we live and make our choices. But we have also been affected by outside forces such as government, advertising and the media.

'I would like to try an experiment with one of you, and I would like to work out who is best suited. In a moment I will make a series of statements or questions, and I want you each to consider if any of them applies to you. If you would answer yes, then I want you to raise your hand. Understood?'

They all nod and you begin, making notes of all their responses rather furtively in your notebook as you go.

'I am middle class.'
'I am not easily influenced.'
'I was brought up locally.'

'I consider myself to be well adjusted.'

'I earn an average wage.'

'I would not go on a package holiday to Ibiza.'

'I work hard to provide for my family.'

'I make my own choices.'

Spend a few moments considering the various responses noted in your book.

'OK, I will use Michelle for this experiment. The three leading brands of washing powder in this country are, as you probably are aware, Sudso, Shine and Wave 3. I wonder, given the choice of those three, which you would select. Name your choice NOW!' You snap your fingers and she responds, 'Shine.'

'A very interesting choice,' you say, as you remove a white card and lay it on the table. On it is a short paragraph that reads:

Market research has shown that in your locality the majority of middle-class adults tend to choose Shine in preference to Wave 3 or Sudso.

Your audience seems impressed!

'You see, we are all influenced by advertising. Having decided which of you was the most typical "target" for advertisers, it was for me, at worst case, an even bet. And by the way, Michelle, do not be concerned that your thoughts are being read. It was for me simply a gamble. But I wonder whether, if we take it to the next level, we can do something even more impressive.'

Remove from your pocket three different chocolate bars: a Nutty Bar, a Mint Crème and a Chocco Bar. Lay them in a line in front of Michelle.

'In that last experiment I saw a very direct response to advertising in your choice. But washing is a necessity, and so the advertisers like to keep their influence constrained to the more rational part of your brain. More frivolous choices are often influenced by subtle forces working on an emotional level, in a way in which we do not understand. Listen carefully, please.

'We are going to make an indirect choice of one of these three chocolate bars. Please, raise both arms and point your index fingers towards the table. Now close your eyes, please. Now slowly lower your fingers and touch one bar with each finger, then push those two bars aside, leaving you with, open your eyes, the Mint Crème.'

Direct Michelle to turn over the card to reveal a further message…

Further research shows that females who use Shine tend to have an emotional connection with creamy confectionery such as Mint Crème – although externally they may express a preference for other bars.

◎ ◎ ◎ The Secret ◎ ◎ ◎

Even though the method behind this trick at first seems simple and straightforward, it is in fact very powerful because a number of methods are used to cloak each other. (I'll explain more about that in the 'Final Thoughts' section.) There are several components involved in this trick, including a force, time and verbal misdirection, and two sets of 'multiple outs' (see box below).

Let's start with the choice of products. In my example, I have chosen washing powders and chocolate, but you could use any products you like. I feel these two products work well, however, because they are among the most heavily advertised commodities. (Furthermore, the examples I have given are not, as far as I am aware, actually real brands. You should use brands that are popular in your home country or region.)

Once you have chosen your products, you need to write out your prediction card, or should I say, 'cards', as there are in fact three of them! They are all almost identical. On one side they should read something like the first prediction we revealed about the choice of washing powder. Each one should state a different preference of product. Also, I suggest you replace the words 'in your locality' with the name of your home town, city or county. Place each

Multiple Out

A 'multiple out' is a fantastic tool in the mind magician's repertoire. This is where you have several potential variations to the ending of your trick; you base the decision as to which ending to choose on your audience's selections or choices.

To understand why it works, you need to remember just one fact: your audience has no idea what is going to happen next in your trick, so when they see you pull out an envelope containing a prediction, they think you have performed a miracle. What they never know is that you have several other predictions waiting in different places!

of these three cards in a different pocket, and make sure you can easily remember which is where.

The other sides of the three cards should again contain almost identical messages. This time the choice of chocolate bar remains the same, but the words 'females who use Shine' naturally needs to match up to the choice of powder on the other side of the card. Mentioning the other two bars as possible choices in the message is important to keep in, as Michelle may indeed have had a preference for one of the others. But we have wrapped this up in some psychological intrigue.

And so I am sure you now know how the first part works. They name their choice and you simply dip into the appropriate pocket and remove the card with their choice on it. But it is not as simple as that. There are two or three things you need to do to make sure it goes smoothly and that the effect is sold.

First, when you ask helper to choose one, it is imperative that you use similar words to 'Given the choice of these three, which would you choose?' If you simply said, 'Which powder would you choose?' they may name another brand entirely. You need to ensure they choose from those three only. A second most critical point is to recall which pocket the required card is in and to be able to get to it and withdraw it smoothly without looking at what you are doing. At this point you should maintain eye contact with your audience. If they suspect you are thinking about what you have to do, your cover is blown. Finally, make sure you lay the card down, ensuring they don't as yet get a chance to see what is written on the reverse.

So far we have made an accurate prediction, and have set up another

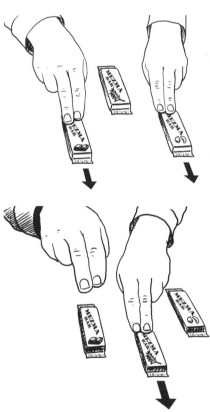

prediction for the chocolate bar we are in fact about to force. Let us assume that we want to force the Mint Crème bar, as in our example. Lay the three bars out in front of your helper, with the Mint Crème in the middle. Have them raise their hands, point downwards, close their eyes, lower their fingers and touch two of the bars. If, as in the example, they touch the other two bars, simply say, 'and push the other two away, leaving you the Mint Crème'. But it is essential to remember to make your words flow almost as if it is one sentence that you had intended to say from the outset. The best way to achieve this is to speak slowly and methodically, without a hard rhythm.

But what if one of the bars they touch is the Mint Crème? In this case, just carry on and say, 'Now push them forward and lift one finger to make another choice …' Now you have two possibilities. If they lift the finger touching the other bar (leaving them touching the Mint Crème), you say, 'leaving you with your choice, the Mint Crème'. If they release the finger touching the Mint Crème, say, 'and your choice was the Mint Crème'.

You are probably wondering what the meaning was of all the questions and statements you asked and made at the start of the trick. The answer is that it was all meaningless verbiage to throw your audience off the scent.

◉ ◉ ◎ Final Thoughts ◎ ◉ ◉

The main lesson that this trick teaches us is that simplicity can work well if used correctly. One essential element to the trick's success is that you do not actually claim it as a trick. It is 'research' – you are simply demonstrating what advertising companies have spent millions working out how to do. We also learn that we need to be confident with the delivery of our words. We must choose our words carefully, quickly and seamlessly.

The most powerful part of this trick, however, is how the second part sells the first. I had chosen a female to help not because she was suitable psychologically, but because my prediction centred on a product advertisers might categorize as a typical female choice. This not only makes the trick more personal, but also reinforces the scientific angle, even more so when we restate the original prediction. When the viewer tries to reconstruct his or her experience, it will be as if you knew all along – well, of course you did!

RUNHALLE

For millennia people have had a deep fascination with the art of fortune-telling, and this is a subject about which I have written many times before. While I do believe in the art, I am also aware of how careful one must be, if receiving (or indeed, giving) readings, to not fall into one of the many traps that lie in wait.

For example, I was discussing the subject recently with a happy couple who had been married some 20 years and were still blissfully in love. She told me the story of how she had seen a tarot-card reader who told her she would meet a tall, dark stranger, in London, and that he would be the love of her life. She went to London a week later and met her husband! Was this truly a prophecy, or had she been influenced into seeking tall, dark men and made an extra effort to get to know them – a kind of self-fulfilling prophecy? The following little trick with a fortune-telling theme plays on this very idea.

◎ ◎ ◎ You Will Need ◎ ◎ ◎
- A couple of helpers
- A bag of rune stones – secretly prepared
- A sheet of paper on which the stone meanings are explained
- A card and a pen

◎ ◎ ◎ The Trick ◎ ◎ ◎

You are still with Jon, Sandra and Michelle.

'There is much more to influence than simply the choices we make. Perhaps we have influence over others, or even the world around us. I don't know if any of you have ever seen these before?'

Remove a bag of rune stones and empty them onto the table in front of you. Lay out a sheet of paper on which the stones and their meanings are briefly explained. Give your helpers a few moments to cast their eyes over them.

Look Jon in the eye and ponder for a moment before writing something on a card. Turn your attention to Sandra and write something else on the card, which you then fold up and hand to Michelle for safekeeping.

'These rune stones stem from an ancient Norse tradition, when they were used as a means of determining the right time to go to battle or to sow crops. Most decisions that the ancient warriors and farmers made were based upon casting the runes.

'From time to time, they would play a game to determine each other's character, and would sometimes decide upon suitable leaders and candidates for other important jobs based upon the result. The game was called Runhalle (rune-hall-ah), and I think we should play it now.

'Jon, you may go first. What you should do is gather all the stones in your hands, then let them gently fall onto the table randomly. You will see some have fallen facing downwards and some facing upwards. I will remove the face-down ones for you. Now, please, cast the stones again.'

He does this several times until only one stone remains face upwards, which you push to one side. You then hand the stones to Sandra and have her do exactly the same until she is left with one stone.

'Jon, let us look at the stone you have selected. I see you have been left with the stone known as "Kanu". This is a stone of inspiration that sees us through adversity, as we are able to lead ourselves and others out of the darkness and into the light. You like to be the one who helps others; you are strong but caring. I am sure from what I know of you, Jon, that this is relevant to you. Am I correct?' He nods and you turn your attention to Sandra.

'This is a very interesting stone, Sandra. It is known as "Joy". This stone tells us we have a right to enjoy the fruits of our labour and that we should not be ashamed about taking a little pleasure when we can. This is the stone of a true Earth Mother. Does this mean anything to you?' She seems to concur with what the stone is telling her and smiles.

'The real question is, were these stones chosen by pure luck, or did fate have a hand in it? Even more interesting is the possibility that you recognized a few key words that meant something to you in the descriptions that I showed you earlier. Given that connection, have you then subconsciously directed yourself to select a stone of relevance to yourself? Of course, I could simply be making these descriptions fit, but there is evidence that I did nothing of the kind!

'I, too, see these connections. You may recall I wrote something down before.' Ask Michelle to unfold the card you gave her. Upon it are drawn two rune stones, Kanu and Joy, and beneath them the names Jon and Sandra.

◎ ◎ ◎ The Secret ◎ ◎ ◎

The basic method to this trick is simplicity in itself. Having said that, it is incredibly deceptive. I have often used this trick, or a version of it, in my professional work.

The first items we will need are some rune stones. These can be easily purchased at new-age shops and in some bookstores, along with a book describing their meanings. They typically come in a nice soft bag, which makes a great magical prop.

You need to modify two of the stones. In my example it was Kanu and Joy, but I suggest you read through the meanings of the stones for yourself and make up your own mind as to which definitions will likely give you the most mileage. The modification is simple, but it needs to be done with great care. Take a good look at your stones and see how the symbols are marked or engraved upon them. Often they are carved out with a shallow groove, then painted with a contrasting colour. Simply put, you must make your chosen stones double-sided so that they will never fall face down.

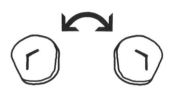

Finally, you need a sheet of paper with pictures of the stones and a brief meaning or description to show your helpers at the outset. You can copy the description from the booklet that comes with your stones, but whatever you do, try to write it on nice-looking paper or parchment.

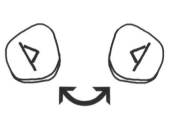

To set up the performance, put the Kanu stone in the bag along with the other rune stones, keeping the Joy stone hidden in your pocket. Make sure it is easily accessible, as we don't want any fumbling around. Begin by introducing the stones to your helpers. Show them the sheet with the meanings, and perhaps point out one or two of the stones to them; you can even give them some to examine more closely. Explain that you would like your first helper to hold the stones in his hands, then drop them onto the table. This is a very nervous moment for him, as he will be scared about dropping them, and even about making too much noise. This is a perfect time for a bit of subterfuge on your part.

Casually, without making any fuss, and especially not mentioning the fact, put your hand in your pocket and take out the Joy stone. Keep your hand closed and allow it to fall to your side. Look at the stones that have now been cast, and with your other hand start to collect a few of the stones that are face down. When you have five or six, pass them into your other hand, which is, of course, holding the Joy stone. Repeat the casting process until Kanu is forced on your first helper. Now hand all the remaining stones, including Joy, to your second helper, and have that person cast the stones.

Once that is done, put the stones back in the bag, leaving the two forced stones on the table for a moment. As you describe the meaning of each stone, pick it up and point out the design to your helper. This is to help them to remember it, as you will then put the two force stones away safe and sound in the bag. You ask for your prediction to be shown, and you have performed a double miracle.

What's more, you have even got away with a simple sleight of hand!

◎ ◎ ◎ Final Thoughts ◎ ◎ ◎

This trick does not have to be performed as an example of 'influence'. As I have already indicated, all of the tricks in this book could be turned into examples of mind reading, control or influence – how you want to perform each trick is up to you.

Rune stones are very beautiful, but they don't always come cheaply. If you prefer, you could make your own set out of small, flat stones or perhaps just use pieces of wood. Another option is to do this trick using coins – make up a set of 15 to 20 mystical symbols of your own, and draw them on coins using an indelible marker. Make sure you draw them on a mixture of the heads and tails sides, as this will help to throw your audience off the scent.

CHAPTER 4:
ANYTHING YOU CAN DO . . .

Although there are only two tricks in this chapter, I feel it is one of the most important sections of the book, as it contains an essential lesson on how to change the pitch of a trick, thus rendering it entirely different.

There is an old saying that goes something like this: 'You have no greater power than when you give it away.' I am not sure where this saying originated, but it has been used and reused to encourage leaders, generals and managers to allow their subordinates to feel they have a voice – even if they don't really have a say and are simply being misled. In this chapter, we are going to apparently give our helpers the power to read minds, and to use the 'hidden powers' that we all possess. The reality, however, is that you, the performer, are in complete control all along – it is you who calls the shots.

This could, of course, be considered a risky strategy. If our spectators can pull off miracles equal to ours, then what is our purpose as a performer? Why are we being paid to do what anyone else can do? The answer really lies in assuming the role of an enabler. Almost certainly our helpers have not done anything quite like this before; they have no experience or skill in this area. Without some external assistance, how on earth could they even begin to read minds?

Take a backward step and see how our audience perceives a trick in which someone from the audience performs a miracle. At one level, you will appear a better, more gracious person to them for sharing the limelight. At worst, some of them will simply put what happened down to your trickery, which is, of course, the truth! Some will actually believe it was your helper who had the special powers. But the majority will think, 'Wow, he is clever! He can even make other people read minds!'

Here are two examples of such power sharing for you to enjoy.

STOOGE FRIGHT

No one can learn a new skill and become a master at it in an instant. Everything worth doing in life requires effort and, perhaps, a bit of practice. If we are going to share our mind-reading power with someone, we need to start off simply with an easy exercise, and then slowly work up to something really powerful.

It is also worth remembering that mind magic should not be taken as a deadly serious subject. You need to have some fun with it, and when you do, your demeanor actually helps to make it more real.

The first trick in this chapter has a slight comedic element leading up to a miraculous revelation. Enjoy!

◎ ◎ ◎ You Will Need ◎ ◎ ◎

- Two helpers – the more gullible the better!
- A pack of playing cards – with one 'special' card

◎ ◎ ◎ The Trick ◎ ◎ ◎

You are joined by your old friends, Graeme and Andrew, who have asked to see some mind magic.

'You know, you have always struck me as the kind of person who could do a little mind reading, Andrew. Let's try an experiment.'

Open a pack of cards and begin shuffling. 'I want you to choose a card for me, Graeme. I will flick through the cards and, when you wish, please call out for me to stop.'

Run your thumb along the edge of the cards and split the pack in two at the point where Graeme calls out. 'Your card is this one immediately below where you stopped. Please look at the card, then reassemble the deck and give it a thorough shuffle.'

Graeme takes the lower half of the deck, looks at his card, then takes the upper part and shuffles everything together. Take the deck from him for 'safety'.

'Now, there are 52 cards in this deck and the chances of anyone guessing your card are of course one in 52. Sometimes that happens by chance, but I don't deal in chance. I need absolutes.

'Graeme, please concentrate on your card, and Andrew, look him in the eye and see if you can see a card. As a professional, may I suggest you don't attempt to get the whole card at once. Perhaps go for the colour, then the suit and finally, the number.

'If you focus, you should see the image of a card appear in mid-air around here.' Gesture with your hand in front of Andrew's face.

'Can you see the colour?' He names black. 'Not quite tuned in yet. Please try again.' He names red, of course, then realizes you are holding the deck in the hand with which you are gesturing. On the face of that deck is a card which he realizes is Graeme's.

After a few more moments, he correctly names the card as the five of diamonds. After another moment, Graeme and some other folks watching also realize what you have done and laugh and groan a little.

'No matter. I was teasing you slightly, but I did have a purpose. I made Andrew my unwitting stooge to help him get tuned in for this much more powerful demonstration. Graeme, please choose another card just as before.'

He does this and you instruct him to place the card on top of the deck, cut it into the middle and, if he wishes, to cut the deck a few more times. Take the cards and shuffle them, then hand them to Andrew.

'I would like you to think of a number in the range of 15 to 25, and deal out that number of cards into a pile on the table.' He does as you ask. 'Deal those cards into two piles, putting one card on each in turn.'

When he is done, ask him to lay his hand on one of the piles; he does as you ask.

'Now, we had a little fun earlier, but this is deadly serious. Graeme, will you now for the first time name your card.' It was the two of clubs.

'Andrew, please turn over the card you are touching.'

He lifts his hand from the deck and turns over the top card. It is indeed the two of clubs.

◎ ◎ ◎ The Secret ◎ ◎ ◎

Both phases of this trick utilize an old friend of the magician, the corner short card. With this easy-to-create gimmick you can force cards, locate cards and control them to where you want in the deck. Making a corner short card is very simple, but does require a little care. Your first one may not be perfect, but keep at it until you get it right.

Take a playing card with its face towards you. Trim off about a millimetre of card around the top left and bottom right corners, just as in the picture, right. Now experiment a little. Shuffle your card into the pack. Riffle the corners of the cards with your thumb. You should notice a definite 'click' and a stop as you riffle past the card.

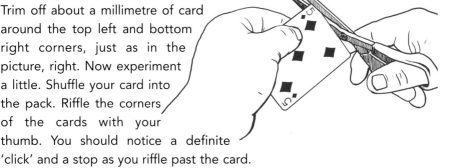

If you hold the deck facing downwards (backs upwards) and riffle up the pack until it stops, you will see that the corner short card is now on top of the lower portion of the deck. That is how you force the first card. In fact, the force card in the trick was our corner short card.

Practise with a friend calling out to you to stop. If you can position the corner short card about two-thirds of the way up the deck, it is an easy matter to slowly riffle through, then lift your thumb up just as your friend calls out. This should bring you up to the corner short card. Work on your timing to make it seem natural and you will have a very convincing force.

Now hold the deck with the cards facing up and riffle through the cards. You will see they stop with the corner short card at the face of the lower

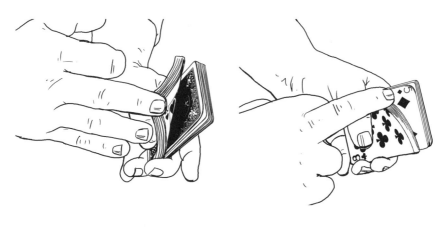

portion of the deck. This is how you get the 'chosen' card to the face of the deck to apparently show to your helper secretly.

Finally, put the corner short card on the top of the deck. Now place another card that you can remember on top of it and cut the deck a couple of times. Hold the deck facing up and riffle down this time. You will now see your other card appear where the deck stops. This is how you locate the second chosen card.

In short, to make this trick work, you simply need to follow these steps:

1. Have the corner short card in the deck about two-thirds up.
2. Explain that you want your helper to call stop.
3. Riffle up through the deck and stop at the corner short card when they call stop.
4. Hand them the lower part of the deck with the corner short card on top.
5. Explain that the top card is their chosen one and to look at it.
6. Hand them the rest of the deck and ask them to shuffle.
7. As you are talking, make a few cuts, riffles and shuffles with the faces up to get the corner short card to the face of the deck.
8. Ask your other helper to 'see' the card – be very blatant about showing him the card.
9. Replace the corner short card on TOP of the deck.
10. Have your helper choose another card while you riffle. This time it is a free choice.
11. Have them place that card on top of the deck (and the corner short card) and cut the cards a few times.
12. As you hold the deck, make some shuffles and cuts, riffle down the deck to bring the second card to the face, and secretly shuffle that card to the top of the deck.
13. Have your helper deal out a number of cards into a pile, then deal these into two piles.
14. Make a note of the last card dealt, as this is the chosen card.
15. Have your helper put his hand on one pile.
16. If he puts it on the chosen card, have it revealed – the trick is over.
17. If he puts it on the other pile, say, 'And push that pile to one side, leaving us with these cards …' and the trick is finished.

These instructions are no doubt a little complex, but in essence we are repeating similar steps a few times to build an effect. Once again, you should practise making everything seem smooth, seamless and consistent.

Final Thoughts

Learning to handle a corner short card takes some practice, but it is worth it, as you can use this gimmick in many ways. I have no doubt you are thinking of some already. Many beginner magicians are concerned that the card looks different from the rest of the pack. Yes, it does, but your audience will not notice, as you will be talking and distracting them with your actions.

One last matter: it is a little known fact that cutting a pack of cards, then completing the cut, doesn't actually change the order of the cards in any way. That is why we were able to have the cards cut a few times after the second card was chosen.

We will be using this concept again later in the book, and I am sure you can make use of it in other ways, too.

MIND SHAPER

You may be familiar with a special set of playing cards known as Rhine cards. These are the ones with a circle, cross, wavy lines, square and star drawn on them. Professor J. B. Rhine and Dr Carl Zener, who were conducting experiments into ESP at Duke University in the 1930s, invented them. These cards are popular with magicians, as there are many tricks you can use them for.

Best of all, there are only five of these cards in a set. So, if you are demonstrating your amazing powers, you already have a head start, as you can get one in five guesses right just by chance. For your delight, here is an experiment using a set of symbol cards you can make up yourself.

◎ ◎ ◎ You Will Need ◎ ◎ ◎
- A helper
- A set of word cards – made up on blank business cards
- A set of illustrated 'prediction' cards – made up on similar card
- A few blank cards
- A pen or pencil

◎ ◎ ◎ The Trick ◎ ◎ ◎

It is now Graeme's turn to see if he can read a mind or two.

'I wonder, Graeme, if you are up for a challenge. Do you think you could read MY mind?

'I have here some cards. There are about 40 or so, I guess. These are not playing cards, however. As you can see, we have words written on each card. Each of these words describes a familiar everyday object.'

Spread out the cards on the table and indeed there are about 40 different items. 'Here, have a good look to make sure that they are truly all different.'

Graeme confirms they are.

'Now, earlier I made a drawing of one of these items, which I have in my pocket. I want you to see if you can tell by reading my mind which of them it is. To make it a little easier, I will narrow it down to just a few of these cards.'

Look through the pack and remove five cards apparently at random, which you hand to Graeme.

'I want you to look through these few cards and try to see into my inner psyche. Try to feel which one I would have chosen and, when you have made up your mind, lay your choice on the table between us, facing downwards.'

He looks through the cards and lays one down, and you lay a similar card that you have taken from your pocket next to it.

Ask Andrew to turn over the card that Graeme chose. 'Very interesting. We see the word HOUSE.' Turn over your card, on which is a picture of a house. Everyone seems impressed.

'Very good, Graeme, but let's try a different challenge. We will use all these cards and you will do it blind!'

Take a few moments to look through the cards – you are apparently choosing a word. 'Good, I have one in mind. I will now draw the object on another card.'

Do as you say and place the card face down on the table. Hand Graeme the cards.

'Now, what I want you to do is to concentrate on my mind and my thoughts. Do not make any hurried decisions; just let an image float into your mind. You will no doubt see many things in your head, and it is not likely that you will see exactly what I have drawn.

'What you should try to do is to make a connection between me and those cards. Deal them facing down onto the table one at a time, and when you feel it is right to do so I want you to stop.'

Graeme pauses for a few moments, then begins to deal the cards slowly onto the table. After he has dealt quite a few cards he stops.

'Are you sure that is where you wish to stop?' He nods and you take the card he stopped at, placing it face down to one side for a moment.

'Let's look at the cards one more time. If you had stopped at the card before, we would have the word DOG and the one after would have been NEWSPAPER. If you had stopped further along, we have CAR, KNIFE and KITE, for example.

'But you stopped at this card. Turn it over, please.'

He turns the card to reveal the word BALL.

'That is very interesting, indeed. Do you know what made you stop at that point?'

He shrugs his shoulders. 'Perhaps you could see into my thoughts and made that connection.'

Have him turn over your card to reveal the drawing you made earlier of – a ball!

◎ ◎ ◎ The Secret ◎ ◎ ◎

There are two secrets to this trick, as you might imagine. One is new to you and the other we have seen before. Both secrets, however, lie in the cards.

You will need to get some blank business cards. These are easily obtainable from stationery shops. On them you need to write the names of some everyday objects. But take special notice, as all is not as random as it seems.

The first five cards should say WALKING STICK, CRUCIFIX, WATER, HOUSE and STAR. These cards also need to be marked on the back (just as in Extra Scentsory Perception on page 30). I suggest you put one dot on the stick, two on the cross, three on water and four on the house. Leave the star blank.

By the way, I have suggested those items because there is a natural code that will help you to recall which marking gives you which word.

Imagine a walking stick. It is one line, and so is marked with one dot. The crucifix is two lines, hence two dots. Three wavy lines reminds us of water, so three dots. The house is a box with four main sides, thus four dots. The star has five points. The only reason we don't mark it is it would look too busy!

You also need five pictures matching the above words to act as your

predictions. Keep them as very basic sketches. They need to be placed in your pockets. Naturally, you need to know how to get to each one easily, and I suggest doing so in the following way.

Place two pictures in your left-hand pocket. These should be the stick and cross, with the stick facing outwards and the cross against your body. Place the wavy lines in a front, middle or top pocket. Finally, place the house and star in your right-hand pocket with the house towards you and the star on the outside. Now think about how you can tell where each card is. Remember our code: it now runs from left to right across your body: one, two, three, four and five; stick, cross, water, house and star.

The remaining 35 or so cards should consist of 18 random words (choose your own to suit) and 17 cards on which are written our force words. These are all words that could be represented by the same drawing. Some good words to use are:

RING
BALL
MOON
SUN
PIZZA
COIN
CD
CIRCLE
PLATE
WHEEL
FLYING SAUCER
CRYSTAL BALL
HULA-HOOP
DISC
CRUMPET
LIFEBOUY

Or, you might like to think of some others. One thing to make sure you do not do, however, is to use any similar words for the rest of the cards. Make a small dot in the middle of each of these force cards.

Now you need to set the deck up for performance. The cards should alternate through the pack, so every other card is a force card. Finally, take the five other cards (stick, cross and so on) and place them randomly throughout the deck.

To perform, introduce the deck of word cards. Spread them for all to see, and point out that they consist of the names of 40 or so everyday objects. For the first phase, go through the cards to choose a few for your helper to select from. You might want to 'um' and 'er' a little, as you apparently choose cards at random. Actually, you remove the first five cards – those matching the predictions in your pocket.

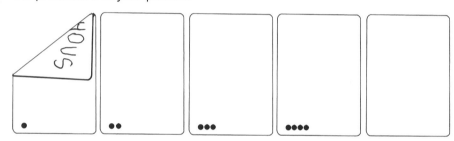

Have your helper select one of those five cards and lay it face down on the table. Make a note of the mark and go straight to the pocket where the prediction matching the card is located. Remove the card from your pocket and place it down on the table next to their choice. (This is something I recommend you practise thoroughly, until it is completely natural.) Then you can reveal the prediction matches their choice.

For the second phase, apparently look through the cards, then draw your choice (a simple circle) on another card. Have your helper deal the cards onto the table until they feel like stopping. Once they stop, there will be a force card either on top of the pile on the table or on top of the cards in their hand. You will be able to tell from the marking. Wherever that card is, reach over and take it, placing it to the side and saying, 'You stopped at this card, but let's look what you would have stopped at had you gone one card further.' Go through a few of the cards on either side, naming them. Of course, do not name any of the other force cards or you might give the game away.

Finally, have them turn over their choice, and you can then show your prediction matches.

◎ ◎ ◎ Final Thoughts ◎ ◎ ◎

The reason I suggest you keep your drawings on the five predictions very basic is because they will match the look of the final prediction. For example, if I had drawn a detailed house for the first phase, your audience might not buy the fact that a simple circle was a pizza. They would expect more detail, so keep everything simple and consistent.

A good verbal diversion when performing a trick such as this is to be deliberately careless and nonchalant about what you are doing. If you are too precise in your instructions they might expect a more accurate result. So play it all slightly off-hand.

You may ask why we didn't shuffle these cards. Well, they are not playing cards – do we need to? They have, after all, been shown to be random, and the more you, the magician, handles these cards, the more this piece of mind magic seems like a card trick to your audience.

One final footnote to this trick is that I could have played it just as it is written: the spectator reads my thoughts and makes a connection. That is powerful stuff, but I could just have easily said I was predicting his behaviour, which is still a great trick. Even better, I could have 'controlled' or 'influenced' him to stop at my will, my prediction being my evidence of that. All it takes is a change of script and for you to assume a different role, that of Svengali, seer or enabler.

CHAPTER 5:
...I CAN DO BETTER

One obvious implication of labelling the tricks in this book as 'psychological' is that 'anyone could do them'. They are science and not magic, and thus they are accessible to all. That is, of course, very true, as anyone could buy this book or visit a website, learn how the tricks herein work and, given some practice, perform them reasonably well, even if they realize they are ultimately tricks. Indeed, in the previous chapter we demonstrated how our audience could use their own abilities in the same way as we do.

The concept that mind magic is some kind of understandable science rather than 'unfathomable' magic somewhat takes the shine off the performer. A magician, or indeed any entertainer, does require a little extra something, that 'X factor', to lift him or her out of the ordinary. So mind magicians need to 'up the ante' and find another way to make themselves look special. The obvious route for this would be for them to prove, or at least appear to prove, that they have greater control over their minds and bodies than the average person. This becomes their magic, their unique factor, the thing that makes them special and enables them to perform the miracles that they do.

In this chapter, we are going to explore a few examples of how you can give the impression of having a well-honed and disciplined mind. The feats we will look at must not be performed or perceived as 'tricks'. They are very much demonstrations of your superhuman abilities and, as such, they are no less impressive to your audience than the greatest trick in the world.

I have to say that the tricks in this chapter will require practice of a somewhat different kind. You will need to sharpen your mental skills to pull them off, but I know you can do it!

MEMO-RANDOM

One of the greatest and most impressive feats I can recall seeing on television as a child was a man who could quickly memorize lists of hundreds of items and recall them on demand from his audience. It certainly seemed impossible, until I learned how to do it myself. It is a skill that can be learned relatively easily, but requires a lot of practice to maintain.

Memory champions compete with each other to see who is best, and one of the tests they often use is to memorize the order of one or more decks of cards. Here's how you can replicate that feat using a little trickery.

◎ ◎ ◎ You Will Need ◎ ◎ ◎
- Two helpers
- A specially prepared pack of playing cards

◎ ◎ ◎ The Trick ◎ ◎ ◎

Justin and Terry join you at the table. The others are watching intently.

'I hope you have enjoyed and been impressed by what I have shown you so far. What I would like to do now is give a short demonstration of exactly how I am able to do these things.'

Take the pack of cards you have been using out of its box, and spread them face up across the table.

'You see in this pack of cards a completely random order. There is neither rhyme nor reason why this card should be next to the other or why that card should be next to its neighbour. And if I shuffle the cards…'

Pick them up, give them a brief overhand shuffle and spread them on the table once again.

'We have a completely different yet equally random order before us.

'This is a good model for the human psyche, which is a chaotic assembly of definite thoughts and memories, mixed with random aspirations and ideas. My particular skill is to be able to make sense of this confusion. Here, let me demonstrate.'

Shuffle the cards and lay them in front of Justin, and ask him to cut the cards at random and complete the cut by placing the lower half of the deck on top of the upper portion. Ask Terry to do the same, then ask if anyone else wishes to cut them. Everyone seems happy to let you proceed.

You notice Justin is wearing a watch with a second hand.

'Justin, I want you to help me with this. I am going to try to commit the order of this shuffled deck to my memory. My personal record is 20 seconds; I would like to get that to 17 or 18 today. When you say "now", I will spread the cards in front of me and will then close the pack up again when I think I have them stored.'

Spread through the cards once Justin gives you the signal, quietly muttering the names of the cards to yourself. After a few moments, close the pack and lay it face down on the table. According to Justin, you took just 16 seconds. Have Justin cut the cards one more time, then have him turn over the top card.

'This card, the three of spades, is my marker – my starting point. I will now turn my back on you and call out the cards in the order in which I remember them. If I get it right, say nothing; if I make a mistake, let me know and I will try to get back on track.'

Turn your back and begin naming cards. 'Six of diamonds, nine of clubs, queen of hearts …' and so on for a few cards.

Pause before saying, 'OK, put the next two down; I will come back to them. I see the four of diamonds, seven of clubs and ten of hearts, and the two I missed were the ace of spades and the jack of hearts.' Pause for a drink of water. 'This is tougher than I thought, but I will keep going.'

'I see the three of diamonds and king of spades, and the next three I see are the queen of clubs … no, spades … two of diamonds and five of clubs.'

Continue naming cards in twos and threes until there are just four left.

'And our final cards are the king of hearts, ten of clubs, four of spades and seven of diamonds!'

Take your well-deserved round of applause.

◎ ◎ ◎ The Secret ◎ ◎ ◎

There are three elements that make this trick work effectively.

There is certainly a little memory work, but there is no need to remember 52 cards – just one word and one number. There is also the fact that cutting the cards never changes the order, as we have already learned. Finally, you must practice to make the memory-work look so easy that you throw your audience off track.

The memory-work enables you to remember the order of the deck. It is, in fact, in a pre-set order using a system known as a 'stack'. There are many stacks in use by magicians, but the one we are using is attributed to a famous and long-dead magician called Si Stebbins. With this or another stack, you can easily work out which is the next card in the deck. So, if you know the top card, you can know the next and the next and so on.

Simply put, the value of the next card in the deck is three more than the current one. Of course, we need to bear in mind that the ace has a value of one, the jack 11, the queen 12 and the king 13. So, if our top card is an ace, its value is one, and so the next card is four, the next seven, the next ten, the next 13 (which is a king). The next card cannot be valued at 16, so we start again from zero and our next card is a three, then six, then nine, then 12 (which is a queen). If we count three one more time, we pass zero, taking us to two, five, eight and finally 11 (which is the jack).

But we must also randomize the suits and we use a code word, CHaSeD, which is an acronym for clubs, hearts, spades and diamonds. So, if we start with the ace of clubs, the next card is the four of hearts, the next seven of spades, then ten of diamonds, round to the king of clubs and three of hearts and so on.

The full stack is shown in the table below. But rather than having you assemble the stack by copying the table, I want you to practice setting up the stack by memory using your key number and key word: three and CHaSeD. This will help you to learn the structure of the stack more quickly.

Si Stebbins Stack

3S	6D	9C	QH	2S	5D	8C	JH	AS	4D	7C	10H	KS
3D	6C	9H	QS	2D	5C	8H	JS	AD	4C	7H	10S	KD
3C	6H	9S	QD	2C	5H	8S	JD	AC	4H	7S	10D	KC
3H	6S	9D	QC	2H	5S	8D	JC	AH	4S	7D	10C	KH

Now you can see how, if you know one card, you can go through the rest of the deck naming the cards one by one. But how did our stack survive the deck being shuffled and cut many times? The shuffle is, of course, a false one (see page 28). And, as we have already seen, cutting does not change the order of the cards – just the start and end points. (You can use a stacked deck to demonstrate this. Cut off about half from the top of the pack and lay it on the table. Put the bottom portion on top of it, then spread the cards in front of you. See how your stack is still intact.)

The final element that makes this trick work is to not call the whole deck out in order. Not only would that be boring, but some audience member might detect that the sequence of suits is repeating. Go back to my description of the trick, looking at the order of the cards in comparison with the stack. You will see that I used a number of diversionary tactics.

Finally, you will have noticed that I missed out a couple of cards and then went back to them. This causes a break in the suit sequence. I also called out cards in twos and threes, breaking the pattern again. Some groups were called in reverse order – again blurring the stack to our spectator's view. And I miscalled a couple of cards and corrected myself – this has the double benefit of masking the stack and making it look as if I am not reading a script. Finally, I named the last few cards backwards and mixed up, for a grand finale. In order to do this last part, you really do need to learn the stack by heart. It will take some practice, but the result is well worth the effort.

◎ ◎ ◎ Final Thoughts ◎ ◎ ◎

You may have noticed in the description of the trick that I implied this was the deck we had used for a previous trick, further removing the possibility in our spectators mind that the deck was in any way pre-arranged. Of course, it was not the same deck, but you can easily create that impression by subtly switching two decks. This idea can apply to any trick and requires no sleight of hand or skill other than a little confidence.

All you need are two decks: one arranged, the other regular. Place them both in your jacket pocket. Perform a trick with the regular deck and put it away in the pocket. Perform another trick without cards, then say something like, 'I would like to show you something else with these cards…' and pull out the arranged deck. Do not say, 'I will get the same deck out again,' as that is a surefire signal you are up to something.

There are many tricks in which stacked decks are used, but don't bother to learn lots of different stacks – one good one should be all you need.

MORE POWER TO YOUR ELBOW

Another group of people who frequently display extraordinary abilities are martial arts experts. Apart from their well-disciplined exhibitions of controlled aggression, they show us how to relax and use natural forces to our advantage. They do many things it is wise not to attempt yourself simply because they do require practice and a controlled environment. Having said that, you could class some of their feats as tricks because quite often they do not require strength or even much practice – just a little-known fact about physics, or the way the human body reacts.

A good mind magician ought to have much in common with these trained experts. Here are a few examples that demonstrate the power you have over your body and the bodies of your helpers.

◎ ◎ ◎ You Will Need ◎ ◎ ◎

- Two helpers – preferably the same gender as you, and of similar stature
- A little bit of secret knowledge

◎ ◎ ◎ The Trick ◎ ◎ ◎

Stand up and move away from the table and have Terry and Justin join you.

'One of the abilities one learns when doing my kind of magic is how to channel energy very effectively. With a little practice, you can even sap another person's strength. Here, let me demonstrate.'

Stand with your right arm pointing away from your body, with the palm of your hand facing upwards. Ask your helpers to stand in exactly the same way as you.

'In a moment, Terry, I will try to bend your arm upwards. Your job is to prevent me from doing so. You will need to focus on your arm and me pushing against you, and resist as much as you can. I will count down from five to enable you to prepare yourself.'

As you count down, Terry obviously tenses his body and you simply walk up to him and place your left hand in the crook of his elbow and your right under his wrist, and you easily and swiftly bend his arm.

'Now, that was too easy. Please try again a little harder!'

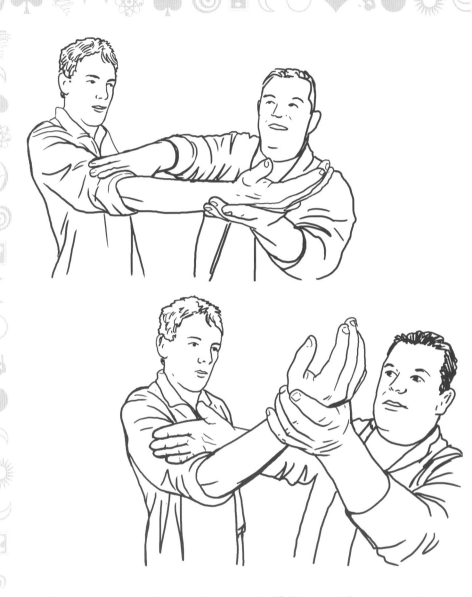

Repeat your countdown and once again lift his arm with consummate ease.

'Now, Terry, this might be considered a little unfair, as you are just a little shorter than me. Let's try with Justin who must be ten centimetres taller.'

This time Justin prepares himself, and just as before you bend his arm without any problem whatsoever.

'And just to prove that this doesn't just happen every time, you guys can try it with me!'

Hold your arm out. Terry tries first to bend it with no success. Justin has a go and, just like Terry, he fails to move your arm, despite all his efforts.

'You see, guys, I have the power to control strength, both my strength and yours. I can give you the power to move things and can just as easily take it away.

'Let's try something else.'

Have Justin and Terry stand on either side of you, and each grab an arm below the elbow with two hands.

'On the count of three, I want you both to lift me in the air. One, two, three!'

They manage to lift you several inches off the ground, then place you firmly back onto the floor.

'Now I will attempt to remove your strength.'

Face Justin directly and look him in the eyes. Touch each of his forearms gently, and pull your hands away sharply. Repeat this process with Terry.

'Now your strength is gone. Let us try once more.'

Take your positions exactly as before, and count to three. Terry and Justin try to lift you as before, and yet despite all their huffing and puffing your feet remain planted firmly on the ground.

As you finish, snap your fingers to allow their strength to return.

◎ ◎ ◎ The Secret ◎ ◎ ◎

Both of these demonstrations share pretty much the same secret. It is the power of relaxation and channelling your strength effectively that makes this work. If you know anything about martial arts, you will perhaps know that practitioners often talk about using other people's energy against themselves. In a way I guess this is what we are doing here.

Have a friend nearby who can help you to practise. First, stand with your arm out as described, with the palm upwards. Tense your body and especially your arm. Have your friend place a hand inside your elbow and the other under your wrist, and have them try to lift. Do all you can to resist, and you will see that your energy works against you and they can move your arm with no effort.

Now try it again, but this time relax; do not fight their energy.

Imagine your arm reaching out from your body, and try to visualize it with energy flowing out of the end like a ray of light, perhaps. You could also try 'seeing' your arm reach out towards a distant mountain which will support you. Allow your arm to bend slightly. Keep the images in your mind, and you will see that this time your friend will not move you as easily. With practice, you will be able to keep your arm perfectly straight.

The double arm lift works in very much the same way. Again, have some friends help you to practise. The only thing to remember is that they must hold your arm below the elbow. Hold your arms stiff, and let them try to lift you. If they are relatively fit, they should do so successfully.

Now try it with you relaxing. Shake your arms a little to loosen them up, and visualize yourself holding onto some very heavy weights, one in each hand. Have your friends try again, and you will see once more it is much harder for them to lift you.

You can learn to accentuate the effect on your helpers by altering their experience of the moment they can lift you slightly. Tense yourself as you prepare to be lifted, and imagine you are a coiled spring that is released as they lift you. This makes the lift a whole lot easier for them the first time and dupes them into trying with the same or even less effort the second time.

◎ ◎ ◎ Final Thoughts ◎ ◎ ◎

There are many tricks from the world of martial arts that you can adapt for yourself, but they do take practice and a little care. For example, if you are short and slightly built, and you have a body builder try to bend your arm and lift you, there is a chance he may hurt you in the process. So, if possible, choose your helpers to be of roughly, but not exactly, the same stature as you.

MATHS DESTRUCTION

I have always had a love of numbers. So much so that as a teenager I actually asked my maths teacher at school to give me extra lessons and homework. The ability to manipulate numbers well has always been a godsend. From my early days as a darts player right up to my present career as a magician, I have put my numerical skills to good use.

With a little effort, you, too, can put on a demonstration of rapid calculation, and so here I offer you a two-part routine that seems to get more impossible at each stage. You'll need to work at it – but as always, the prize makes it worthwhile.

◎ ◎ ◎ You Will Need ◎ ◎ ◎

- Two helpers – any adults with at least an average understanding of maths will do
- Two notepads and two pens
- A calculator – not for you, but for your helpers to prove what you have done
- A blackboard or flip chart and some writing materials

◎ ◎ ◎ The Trick ◎ ◎ ◎

Phase 1 – It All Adds Up

'Of course, having a good memory and great control over your body requires a sharp mind. I would like to show you how well I have mine trained.'

Hand Terry a notepad and pen, and take a similar pad and pen for yourself.

'I want you to listen carefully to the following instructions. In a moment, I am going to ask you to write down a four-digit number, which you will name aloud. Once you have done that, I want you to write down a second four-digit number made up of the same digits, but scrambled up. You can also name that number. Do you understand so far? Good.

'Then I want you to subtract the smaller from the larger number. Take the result and add the digits of that answer together. This will probably give you a two-digit number. Please add those together again, and keep adding until you have one digit left. Is that all clear?'

Go over it one more time, and offer him the use of a calculator if he needs it to assist with his addition.

He announces his first number as 4876 and the second as 7684 – you then shout, 'GO!'

You both begin scribbling furiously on your pad. Terry fiddles with the calculator, but just after a second and a half you place a piece of paper face down on the table and discard your pad. You begin to look impatient as it takes Terry a minute or so to complete his sums. He indicates that he is finished, and you ask him to name the final digit, which is nine.

'That took you about eighty seconds, I believe. That is not bad, as I did put you under some pressure. But you may have noticed that I wrote my answer in just over a second. That is because I have a very sharp mind!'

Turn over your less-than-two-second answer; it is nine – just the same as Terry's 80-second answer!

Phase 2 – No Fibbin'

'I wonder if you have seen that movie where they need to unlock a bank vault – the secret code was a special number called a "Fibonacci sequence".

'It sounds complex, but is actually very simple. All you do is start with two numbers and add them together to make the third. You then add the second and third to make a fourth, and so on.'

Demonstrate on the blackboard by beginning with 1 and 2. Your next number is 1 + 2 = **3**. The next is 2 + 3 = **5**. The next is 3 + 5 = **8**. The next would be 13 and the one after that 21.

'What I would like you to do, Justin, is to create a Fibonacci sequence of let's say ten numbers, and I want you to write them in a descending column on the blackboard. Choose any two different single-digit numbers to start with, and add them up with this calculator as you go, but do not write the total down.

'While you are doing that I will turn my back. Please don't say aloud any of the numbers you write, but do let me know when you have finished.'

You hand him the calculator and some chalk, and he begins scribbling away. After several minutes he tells you he has finished. Turn around so that you can see the list of numbers on the board.

Stroll over, grab the chalk, draw a line under the bottom number and write '836' beneath the line.

'Terry, please check Justin's work. Add all the numbers in his list together for us.'

Terry spends a minute or so tapping on the calculator and eventually announces the answer is indeed 836.

You really do have a super sharp mind!

The Secret

Both of these amazing demonstrations are very easy to perform, and only one of them requires you to think at all. The most important thing is that your helpers understand exactly what is expected of them.

Phase 1

This is so incredibly simple. Try it for yourself.

Write down a four-digit number – let's say 3789, and we scramble that to give 9783. Subtract the smaller from the larger.

$$9783 - 3789 = 5994$$

Add the digits together.

$$5 + 9 + 9 + 4 = 27$$

Add those digits together.

$$2 + 7 = 9$$

Let's try one more example using 7356, which we can scramble to 3657. Subtract the smaller from the larger.

$$7536 - 3657 = 3879$$

Add the digits together.

$$3 + 8 + 7 + 9 = 27$$

Do you have déjà vu right now? The answer will always be nine.

So this demonstration is simplicity itself. Make sure you instruct your helpers carefully to ensure they do things in the right order and in the right way.

When you say go, simply write 9 on your pad, tear off the piece of paper and leave it on the table. Wait 'impatiently' for your helper to struggle through with his maths while you look like a genius!

Phase 2

This part of the trick is also quite simple, but it does require you to do a little bit of mental arithmetic. It is not too onerous, however, given a little bit of practice.

Take a look at the sequence of numbers Justin wrote in our example. The fourth number from the bottom was 76. If you multiply 76 by 11, you get 836.

And that is all you need to do. I suggest you ask your helper to start with two single-digit numbers. This will not only make life easier for him, but also should help to make it easier for you when you have to multiply.

Let's look at another example, just so you can be clear, starting with 5 and 7.

5

7

12

19

31

50

81

131

212

343

Our fourth from bottom number is 81. Multiplied by 11 we get 891, and if we add all the digits we get 891!

◎ ◎ ◎ Final Thoughts ◎ ◎ ◎

Two things spring to mind here. First, that you should choose your helpers carefully. I would love to do many more maths demonstrations in my professional act, but I am wary of doing so. Why? The answer is simple: the teaching and appreciation of numbers is not as deep and widespread as it was, say, 30 years ago. This is not me being a grumpy old man – just accepting that many audience members would not know some of the maths concepts I am talking about, so the impact of my act could be lost.

The other point you might want to consider is using the '9' principle in Phase 1 as a force. Think about how powerful that would be. For example, ask someone to think of a large random number, which is then distilled to a single digit. You then reveal your prediction of the ninth object, the ninth card in a deck or the contents of page nine in a book. Give it some thought and experiment.

CHAPTER 6:
RIGHT FROM THE START

Every entertainment show needs a powerful closer. You have to leave your audience feeling great about your show; leave them feeling that it was all worthwhile. The same is undoubtedly true of a mind magic show, and no matter whether you are simply performing for friends or family, or playing to packed theatres around the world, you need a killer ending. Here I present three very powerful pieces of mentalism, perhaps the strongest effects I have ever offered for publication.

I am not suggesting for a moment you should use all three, although they would make a neat show, but choose one or two. What I think you will find works well is a combination of either 'Datum' or 'Eggs is Eggs', coupled with 'Breaking News' as a final closer.

There is a running theme common to these three effects, that 'you' knew all along what was going to happen or at the very least you have been in total control of events. What's more, with 'Breaking News' you have an interesting choice, as I have suggested two slightly different versions of the presentation. Thus you can play it in its simplest form, or change it just a little creating a wonderful opportunity to re-sell all the tricks in your show one last time for double the effect. So join me in our final foray into the mysteries of the mind!

DATUM

People are always fascinated when you can make personal connections with them and talk about their attributes in a positive manner. You may have heard about a form of fortune-telling or prediction known as numerology, where dates and numbers are added repeatedly to leave a final number that tells us something about our characters. I find it an odd science, not least because our Western date system is an artificial construction, has been changed throughout history and is only one of many in use. However, keeping that theme in our mind, we can create a very personal piece of mind magic, giving us a chance to flatter our audience.

◎ ◎ ◎ You Will Need ◎ ◎ ◎

- Two helpers
- A specially prepared pocket diary (a week-to-two-pages format)
- A credit card-sized calendar (ideally blank on the other side)
- A special 'secret device' – more of which below

◎ ◎ ◎ The Trick ◎ ◎ ◎

Daniel and Emma have joined you for the final segment of your show.

'I don't know how many of you here read your "stars" on a regular basis, but we all know that supposedly our date of birth has some influence on our character and the way we are perceived by others.

'For example, when I walked in here this evening, I picked up a very strong sense from this lovely lady to my left and I wrote something down and put it safely away in my wallet. Could I ask you to confirm three things for me: first, that we have never met; secondly, your name; and, thirdly, your date of birth – but being a gentleman I won't ask you to tell me the year as we all know it was 1988!'

She confirms you have never met previously, that her name is Emma and that her birthday is 16 December.

'Now that is fascinating, a Sagittarian. You see, I am a Leo and that makes for an exciting relationship! But I have something really unusual to show you. I hastily wrote something down on a card earlier – wouldn't it be spooky if

what I had written was your birth date?'

While you are talking, you remove your diary and a card from your pocket.

Everyone nods. Lay the diary on the table and show the card. It is, in fact, a business card-sized calendar. 'There you are: the 16th of December!' Point to the date on the card; the audience groans and chuckles. Yes, the date of her birthday is there, but so are all the 364 other days of the year.

'OK you're not too impressed by that, but, you know, I did sense something about you as I arrived. You see, every day of the year has a birthday card associated with it – a birthday playing card – and I picked up just a hint of the character of *your* birthday card...

'I saw someone bright and colourful, and we can all see that from the way you are dressed this evening. But I also sensed someone who has a fairly strong character and takes no nonsense. Would I be correct about you?' Emma nods.

Open the diary and hand it to Daniel. Ask him to check it and confirm that it has playing cards written totally at random throughout the 365 days.

'Could you now open the diary at the page where we find Emma's birthday, the 16th of December. What card is written there, please?'

Daniel names the jack of diamonds. 'Ahh,' you say. 'Just as I sensed earlier, someone colourful yet powerful!'

Hand Emma the calendar card. 'I know I teased you with that silly joke about the date earlier – and I am sorry about that. But would you slowly turn over the card in your hand for me...?'

Written on the reverse of the calendar card it is the jack of diamonds!

◎ ◎ ◎ The Secret ◎ ◎ ◎

There is a bit of work required to set this trick up, but, as you'll see, it is well worth the effort.

There are two parts to the method of this trick. A secret magician's device known as a thumb writer, or nail writer, and an easy-to-learn system for correlating dates with playing cards.

Thumb writers are available from magic shops. There are many different types, and they are not very expensive. Thumb writers enable you to secretly

DATE	Card Rank	Suit
1	4	Clubs
2	7	Hearts
3	6	Spades
4	9	Diamonds
5	8	Clubs
6	Jack	Hearts
7	10	Spades
8	King	Diamonds
9	Queen	Clubs
10	5	Hearts
11	4	Spades
12	7	Diamonds
13	6	Clubs
14	9	Hearts
15	8	Spades
16	Jack	Diamonds
17	10	Clubs
18	King	Hearts
19	Queen	Spades
20	5	Diamonds
21	4	Clubs
22	7	Hearts
23	6	Spades
24	9	Diamonds
25	8	Clubs
26	Jack	Hearts
27	10	Spades
28	King	Diamonds
29	Queen	Clubs
30	5	Hearts
31	4	Spades

write a few letters on a slip of paper or a card. Using and handling a thumb writer takes a little bit of practice and, because there are so many types, it would be impossible to cover all the options here. I suggest you visit a magic shop (there are some suggestions at the back of this book) and try out a few different types to find one that suits you, and also take some advice from the folks in the shop.

You will also need a credit-card-sized calendar. You know the kind, with 365 dates on one side and, ideally, blank on the other. If you cannot find a blank-backed one (many of them have advertising on the reverse), apply a piece of sticky white vinyl and trim it off neatly.

You will also need a pocket diary with a week-to-two-pages format. If you can find an 'eternal' diary with no year, all the better. On the other hand, you could go the whole hog and make up a new diary every year! (Let's face it, we all get plenty of unwanted diaries at Christmas.) You will need to write the names of 365 playing cards against apparently random dates throughout the diary. In fact, there is a sneaky system for the dates, which is at the heart of this trick.

The hardest work in this effect is going to be setting up the diary, which might take you an hour or so. The second-hardest part will be learning the system, which will take you five more minutes. Practise the handling and timing until it all runs smoothly for you.

Using the table on page 79 as a guide, write the playing cards that are listed against the dates shown. Every month has the same set of cards – except of course our 30-day and 28/29-day months, which simply use fewer entries!

Don't forget that a hidden minority of folks are born on 29 February. If your diary doesn't have that date in it, simply put a note of the date and the card (queen of clubs) in the margin of the last page for February.

The system I have created here is very simple. To perform the trick, you will need to calculate the card for the person's birthday prior to secretly writing it on the calendar. The process is very straightforward:

First establish the VALUE of the card
For ODD dates
Add three to the birthday date to give the value of the card. Thus the 1st becomes a **4**; the 9th becomes a **queen**.

When you get to the 11th, simply ignore the first number ('1'), leaving 1, then add 3 to make **4**. Do the same as you progress through each set of ten days. Thus 11th, 21st and 31st all become **4** and the 13th and 23rd become **6**, and so on.

For EVEN dates

Add five to the date given on the card. Thus the 2nd becomes a **7**; the 10th (which equates to zero) becomes **5**. The same applies as you reach the 20th and 30th, both of which represent a **5**; the 12th and 22nd are **7**; and the 6th, 16th and 26th are all **jacks**.

Now establish the SUIT

We have already discussed the CHaSeD system in this book (see page 65). Just as a reminder, this stands for 'clubs, hearts, spades and diamonds', and is a simple way of remembering a prearranged order of suits. Again, anyone casually looking at the diary will not easily spot this cycle. The 1st in any month therefore is a club, and so are the 5th, 9th, 13th and so on. A little practice with the arithmetic will help you to learn this system quickly.

To establish the card for any given date, first IGNORE the month, as each month is identical – only the day matters. Add 3 or 5 for odd or even, then work the suit out from the CHaSeD cycle. The table on page 79 should make it all clear.

To prepare, put the diary, calendar card and writer in your pocket. Immediately prior to performance, slip the writer onto your thumb. Put your hand in your pocket, and take out the calendar and diary together. The calendar should be underneath the diary, with the blank side facing outwards so that you can write on it.

Ask your helper their date of birth and, while you continue talking, calculate the card for that date and write it on the card. Depending upon how competent you are with the writer, you may write the whole name of the card, or simply put the initials (for example, 'jack of diamonds' or

just 'JD'). Do keep the flow of your patter smooth here, as any stutters or apparent nervousness will signal that you are doing something secretive. So be natural, talk smoothly and gesture with your hands so as to distract attention.

You then display the front side of the calendar. You will no doubt get some groans as this is an 'old joke', but you must move on swiftly.

Invite someone else to examine the diary and see that there are indeed 365 random cards written against the dates. But do not linger too long on this, and after a few moments direct them to turn to the chosen birth date. Have them name the card shown against the date, turn over the calendar card and take your applause.

◎ ◎ ◎ Final Thoughts ◎ ◎ ◎

You will notice from the patter that I used a little bit of 'cold reading' (see page 14), associating the supposed character of my helper with the value of the card. I do this sort of thing all the time, and I am confident enough as a speaker to make my impromptu waffle sound good.

With a bit of practice, you too can get away with waffling like this as long as you follow one simple rule when comparing someone to their chosen card or whatever you do: always be positive and flatter your spectator!

EGGS IS EGGS

One thing magicians of all kinds love to do is to flirt with danger. They may be locked up with a ticking clock signalling an impending falling weight which will crush them if they cannot vanish or escape quickly enough, or they may plunge their arm into a jar containing deadly snakes.

Rest assured that no matter what you have seen a magician do, there is a trick behind it designed to make it safe and sound. Even so, tricks can sometimes go horribly wrong. I recently saw a magician on an 'out-take' television show injure his hand by thrusting down upon the wrong paper cup – he hit the one with the spike in it by accident.

I cannot allow you, dear reader, to put yourself in any such danger. A game of chance seems to be irresistible, however, so I will indulge myself in one that, if it should go wrong, would quite literally leave you with egg on your face!

You Will Need

- A helper
- Six polystyrene coffee cups
- A pair of dice (one of which should be mis-spotted)
- A marker pen
- An uncooked egg
- A special device – more of which later
- A damp cloth – to wipe up afterwards

The Trick

'What I am about to show you all is most definitely not for the faint-hearted! Danger is all around us. We never know when fate will make us step out in front of a car, or deliver a lump of ice straight from an airplane right onto our home. We simply do not know what will happen day to day; in many respects, our lives are a game of chance, and we have little or no influence on the random events that may occur. Or do we?'

On the table in front of you are six polystyrene cups; they are sitting upside down. The cups are numbered one through six.

'Daniel, will you help me with this? I want you to be aware that this is a little dangerous, not for the faint-hearted, as I have already said. But I feel you are the kind of person who likes a thrill – even though I cannot tell you at this stage exactly what the risk is!'

Daniel nods in agreement, and you instruct him to follow your directions to the letter.

Hand him the dice and ask him to roll it; it lands showing number three.

'Now you must take your life in your hands. On the count of three, I want you to slam your hand down onto cup number three. 1 – 2 – 3 – GO!'

There is a dull thud as the cup collapses and Daniel's hand hits the table. The slight air of tension that had been there suddenly dissipates.

'I am not sure why you are all relaxing. There is more to do. Please, roll the dice again.'

It lands on five and, just as before, you ask him to crush cup five. Once again there is nothing inside.

Next time it lands on three again, and so the dice is rolled once more, showing one – there is nothing under that cup either.

Cup two is next, leaving cups four and six.

'Remember, this is not for the faint-hearted, and now your risk of finding something is equal to the risk of remaining unscathed. Do you wish to continue?'

He nods and rolls a six and, just as before, there is nothing inside when the cup is crushed.

'Daniel, you have escaped a most unique and sticky danger by virtue of the luck you have had in throwing this dice, for there is something inside this cup – cup number four.

'But I wonder if you truly believe your throws were entirely random? You see, I could not possibly allow myself to put a helper of mine in any real danger, so I had to exert some influence over you. You may recall, I told you several times this experiment was not "four" the faint-hearted. I really wanted you not to choose number four. NOT FOUR THE FAINT-HEARTED!'

Shout as you slam your hand down onto cup number four. Your audience recoils slightly as the egg that was hiding under the cup explodes, creating just a little mess. 'That is why this game is not "four" the faint-hearted!'

◎ ◎ ◎ The Secret ◎ ◎ ◎

The actual secret to this trick lies with the dice. Stop in at your local magic shop and ask them if they have a mis-spotted die (a die with a number missing). These dice are available with any number missing. A missing number four is obviously ideal for this trick, as it enables you to use the 'not four' patter.

When you get your mis-spotted die, it should also come with a matching die that has all six numbers on it. Place them both in your left pocket, write the numbers one to six on your cups and lay the cups out on the table with an egg under cup number four.

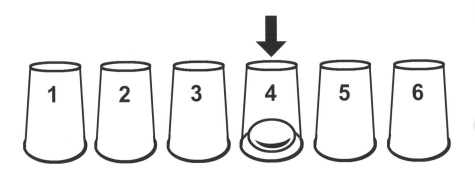

Hand the mis-spotted die to your helper and have him roll it, crushing the cups in turn as the numbers are rolled. Do not be concerned if a number is repeated a few times; this will happen naturally. (If all the numbers were rolled in sequence, your audience would have a right to be suspicious.)

When only one cup is left, pick up the die and toss it up and down a couple of times in your left hand. As you eventually lean forwards to crush the cup with your right hand, drop your left hand into your pocket, dumping the mis-spotted die and bringing out the real one. The noise and flying egg yolk will be enough to distract the audience's attention while you do this. Place this real die on the table should anyone wish to examine it.

Oh, and do make sure you keep a damp cloth nearby to clear up the sticky mess.

◎ ◎ ◎ Final Thoughts ◎ ◎ ◎

This type of 'just chance' effect is very popular with magicians, and they certainly do perform it with all kinds of 'dangers', from spikes to snakes, and all points in between. Eggs for me are a great choice for this trick, as the worst thing an egg can do is get you a little messy, and they are easily cleaned away. You do not have to use eggs, however. You could use anything you wish, but please be mindful of any risks. If you choose to place something sharp or otherwise dangerous under the cup and your helper misheard your instructions, then you would have a potentially career-limiting opportunity. Please take my advice: do not use anything with any real risk attached.

As the cups are crushed, try to build a little more urgency into your patter; this helps to raise the tension leading up to your shout of 'NOT FOUR THE FAINT-HEARTED!' at the climax.

Another take on this trick is to reverse its logic and have something wholly desirable in play. For example, you could have several envelopes, each with a penny in it and one with a large banknote. Alternatively, you could use some keys, only one of which unlocks a special prize of some sort. The choices and possibilities are endless.

BREAKING NEWS

I have already stated more than once in this book that it matters little whether you appear as a mind reader or psychological magician, just as long as you give yourself a definite identity. I am about to break my own rule. In fact, what every magician does (whether he intends to or not) is to raise questions in the minds of his or her audience. Even if the audience can attribute part of the magician's methodology to a 'sleight of hand' or 'psychological influence', a good majority of those in it will leave the show thinking, 'But what about the part where he did that? Surely that's impossible?' Over time, that question about that one part of the show will colour their memories of the whole thing, making it seem even better in retrospect.

This final effect is our closing act. I have given it two possible endings: a simpler one and a more powerful one. I hope that this closing trick will lead your audience to question whether you do really have the power to read minds and see into the future.

◎ ◎ ◎ You Will Need ◎ ◎ ◎

- A helper
- An envelope – prepared in advance
- Another envelope – prepared less in advance
- An evening newspaper – from the day of your performance
- Two sticky labels
- Glue stick
- Pen or pencil

◎ ◎ ◎ The Trick ◎ ◎ ◎

Phase 1

This phase of the trick could be set up at the start of your show, to be performed at the very end (see Phase 2, page 88).

'Joshua, would you please come forward and bring with you the item I sent you in the post. Thank you. Hold it up so that everyone can see it.' He displays an envelope.

'Joshua is acting as your adjudicator today. Last week I sent this letter to

Joshua. He will confirm that it is postmarked from a week ago, and has been in his possession ever since. No one else has been near it, especially me. Is that correct?' Joshua confirms this.

'I also have with me a copy of the evening newspaper for today, which Joshua will look over on your behalf.' Joshua examines the paper and again confirms what you are saying.

'Joshua, I want you to guard your envelope and the newspaper for a short while longer. Please slip the envelope into the newspaper so that it is out of view and out of reach of my hands.' Open the paper, and he slips the envelope in between two pages.

Fold the paper, hand it to him and ask him to make sure that no one tampers with it. Request that he takes his seat again.

Phase 2

The rest of your show passes by with an incredible display of mind tricks and psychological miracles. You take your applause, but then you realize that your audience wants just a little more. Some of them have not forgotten the envelope that you had left with Joshua a bit earlier, and are wondering what it was for.

'Ah, yes. I almost forgot. Joshua, would you please return to the stage and bring the newspaper with you.' He hands you the newspaper and you very gingerly shake it so that the letter falls onto the table.

'Take another look at the envelope, and make sure the magic pixie that lives in the newspaper hasn't tampered with it!' Everybody laughs.

Show Joshua and everyone in the audience the front page of the paper, and ask him to read aloud two or three headlines.

'INTEREST RATES UP TO 5 PER CENT'

'ELEVEN INJURED IN NORTHEAST COACH CRASH'

'LEAGUE LEADERS LOSE 4–0'

Phase 3A

'Joshua, for one final time, please confirm that you have had this letter in your possession for the past week and that nobody has taken it or hidden it from you, and that it most certainly cannot have been tampered with.' He nods. 'Then will you please open the envelope and read the letter inside.'

Dear Joshua,

Thank you for booking to see my show, and for agreeing to help me out this evening. I have clearly marked 'Do not open' on the envelope in which this letter has been placed, so there can be no doubt that it was written over a week ago.

I trust you and your friends have enjoyed the show so far, and that you have been impressed by what the power of the mind can achieve.

To close the show, I would like to offer one final set of predictions as proof of the magical abilities each of us possesses. In the news today, we will all be shocked by a rise in the cost of borrowing, we will see our top team beaten by four goals, and we will be concerned for the welfare of about a dozen people injured on the road today.

Kindest regards,

Marc Lemezma

Take your applause and leave the stage.
As an alternative…

Phase 3B

'Ladies and gentlemen, you may all think that your choices were free ones and your actions random as you have helped me during the show. I wonder if that truly is the case!

'Joshua, for one final time, please confirm that you have had this letter in your possession for the past week, that nobody has taken it or hidden it from you, and that it most certainly could not have been tampered with.' He nods.

'Then will you please open the envelope and read the letter inside.'

Dear Joshua,

Thank you for booking to see my show, and for agreeing to help me out this evening. I have clearly marked 'Do not open' on the envelope in which this letter has been placed, so there can be no doubt that it was written over a week ago.

I trust that you and your friends have enjoyed the show so far, and that you have been impressed by what the power of the mind can achieve. Let us remind ourselves how much a part the six of spades, the four of diamonds and the nine of hearts has played. How I could tell who prefers a Mint Crème chocolate bar over a Nutty Bar. How we recalled memories of houses and pets, and how we made a mess with the egg hiding in cup number four.

To close, I would like to offer one final set of predictions as proof of the magical abilities each of us possesses. In the news today, we will all be shocked by the rise in the cost of borrowing, we will see our top team beaten by four goals, and we will be concerned for the welfare of about a dozen people injured on the road today.

Kindest regards,

Marc Lemezma

◎ ◎ ◎ The Secret ◎ ◎ ◎

Like so many of the secrets of the mind magician, the secret here is very simple, yet oh so powerful. The envelope that is opened and the letter that is read out are not the same ones you originally sent to your helper. You must carefully switch that envelope with a different one, which you must prepare that day as soon as you know what is in the news.

The first things to prepare are two envelopes that are almost identical. Experiment with different types, but you want one that you can easily steam open and reseal without causing any obvious damage or leaving any signs of your tampering.

In one envelope, put a brief letter to your intended helper saying something along the lines of:

I see you were unable to resist the temptation and have looked into the envelope despite my instructions. No matter, I will simply have to perform another miracle on the big night!

Write boldly on the front and across the flap:

'DO NOT OPEN UNTIL THE BIG NIGHT'

Write or print a sticky label with your helper's address on it, and stick it carefully to the front of the envelope. While you are writing that label, make a second identical copy, which you keep for later.

Take a second identical envelope and seal it with nothing inside. Write the 'DO NOT OPEN' instruction in exactly the same place as on the other, and write or print a label with *your own* address on it. Stick it to the envelope, making sure it is in the same position as the label on the first.

Take both envelopes and post them at the same time in the same post box. This means they will be postmarked with the same location, date and time.

It is also a good idea at this point to call your helper to let him know to expect the envelope, to remind him that he is not to open it or tamper with it, and that he should bring it to the show.

On the day of the show, buy the evening newspaper. Make note of some front-page stories, and write out your letter incorporating them. Make sure to date this letter with the date on which you posted the two letters a week or so ago. Carefully open the letter you sent to yourself and place your prediction letter inside. Stick the second address label you made with your helper's address on it over your address, and carefully re-stick the envelope down. Now you have what will look like an identical copy of your helper's envelope.

The final part of the preparation is to smear an inside page of the newspaper with glue stick. Mark the corner of this page with a pen dot, and fold a corner backwards so you can get to that page easily later on. Slip your duplicate envelope into the newspaper (at a different page from the glue!), fold the newspaper in half at the natural crease and you are all set.

When your helper is on stage, show the audience the newspaper fairly freely, but be sure to keep it in your hands. Allow them to see that it is indeed today's edition. Keeping the paper folded, open it up at the glued page by locating the turned-back corner. You may have to peel gently here. Have your helper slip his envelope inside. Lay the newspaper on the table and pat it with your palm firmly a couple of times while saying something like 'I want you to keep this safe for a few more minutes.' Make your pats seem like a positive gesture, to ensure the helper knows what he has to do.

When he returns to the stage at the end of the show, open the paper up carefully; his envelope will stick inside and your duplicate will fall out. Have him confirm that the envelope has not been tampered with. This causes the helper to briefly examine it, confirming that it is the same envelope. However, you must never say, 'Will you verify this is the same envelope?' For as far as the audience is concerned, there is no question that it is indeed the same envelope. If you ask the question, you will inevitably raise doubts and thus undermine your whole act.

Have your helper read the letter aloud and your prediction will astound!

◎ ◎ ◎ Final Thoughts ◎ ◎ ◎

I gave two alternate endings for this effect in an attempt to illustrate how a little extra verbal by-play could enhance the effect immensely. You do have the option of either simply predicting that evening's newspaper headlines, or adding in some predictions of what has already passed in the show. However, simply recounting parts of your show with no specific prediction as part of this trick would be quite a weak effect.

With both letters, you will notice there is a mixture of specific and non-specific predictions. Certainly we have predicted the general tone of the headline, but by saying 'about a dozen' instead of '11', for example, we give credence to that fact this was some sort of vision, albeit one we didn't see with total clarity.

In the second letter we made reference to some of the earlier tricks in this book. You will, of course, need to mention the outcomes of some of the tricks you do yourself. I certainly do not expect everyone to build an act based on my material alone. But when you do write your letter, mention specific cards and numbers that you are going to force, and mix that in with the types of prediction choices that are going to be made.

FURTHER READING

The following is a list of titles that will help you further your knowledge of mind magic.

GENERAL MAGIC BOOKS

Ted Annemann, *Practical Mental Magic*, Dover Publications

Carolyn Boyes, *Body Language*, Collins

Tony Corrinda, *13 Steps to Mentalism*, Robbins Publishers

Karl Fulves, *Self Working Mental Magic*, Dover Publications

Jean Hugard, *Hugard's Magic Manual*, Dover Publications

Richard Jones, *That's Magic!*, New Holland Publishers

Marc Lemezma, *How to be a Mind Magician*, Tobar

Christopher Milbourne, *The Illustrated History of Magic*, Robert Hale

O'Connor & Seymour, *Introducing NLP*, Harper Collins

Mark Wilson, *Complete Course in Magic*, Running Press

OTHER BOOKS BY MARC LEMEZMA (ALL NEW HOLLAND):
Mind Magic

Every Magic Secret in the World Revealed!

The Complete Fortune Teller

USEFUL ADDRESSES

Here are a few addresses of dealers in all things magic, along with some websites, magazines, clubs and societies that may be of interest. I begin with my own website, www.lemezma.com.

MAGIC DEALERS

Alakazam Magic
www.alakazam.co.uk

International Magic
www.internationalmagic.com

Hank Lee's Magic Factory
www.hanklee.com

MAGIC MAGAZINES

Magic Week
www.magicweek.com
Online newsletter updated weekly

Genii Magazine
www.geniimagazine.com

MAGIC CLUBS AND SOCIETIES

There are literally thousands of magic clubs and societies around the world. Here are some details from two of the most prominent, which will no doubt help you locate some magical friends local to you!

The Magic Circle
www.themagiccircle.co.uk

The International Brotherhood of Magicians
www.magician.org

INDEX

Page numbers in **bold** indicate explanations of techniques.

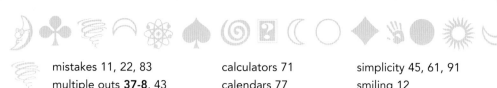